Busy leaders will find the insights in this devotional encouraging, instructive, and uplifting. I'm especially encouraged that all of the wisdom contained here can be traced back to the timeless truths of God's Word. Kudos to Pat Williams for assembling such a useful resource.
JIM DALY/PRESIDENT, FOCUS ON THE FAMILY

I love every book that Pat Williams writes! *The Leadership Excellence Devotional* is no different. It's packed with wisdom and leadership insights for a lifetime.
GRETCHEN CARLSON/CO-ANCHOR, FOX & FRIENDS

I have read many devotional books and written a few myself, but when this one arrived, it so captured me that I finished it that day. No matter your calling in life—sports, business, ministry, politics, getting an education—the material in these pages will enrich you, equip you, and help motivate you to do your job and serve the Lord with joy and efficiency.
WARREN W. WIERSBE/AUTHOR AND FORMER PASTOR AT MOODY CHURCH, CHICAGO

I'm fascinated with outstanding leaders and what makes them great. Pat Williams' new book of leadership teachings should be a lifetime companion for leaders in all fields. This book has given me a huge lift and will do the same for you.
CHRIS BROUSSARD/NBA ANALYST, ESPN

Pat Williams has put together a treasure trove of leadership principles in this wonderful new book. My advice is to read this book regularly, reflectively and reactively. It will make a huge difference in your life.
KIM MULKEY/HEAD WOMEN'S BASKETBALL COACH, BAYLOR UNIVERSITY

Who better to help us craft a game plan for our busy lives than Pat Williams? He spent forty years studying leadership, building winning teams and organizations, and developing strategies. *The Leadership Excellence Devotional* is a must addition to those of us who are attempting to live and lead at the mach 3 speed of life.

JAY STRACK/PRESIDENT AND FOUNDER, STUDENT LEADERSHIP UNIVERSITY

I have read a ton of books on leadership and Pat Williams' new book *The Leadership Excellence Devotional* seems to have summarized them all in a concise manner. Pat not only writes about leadership but is a beacon light to all of us as a true servant leader.

DALE BROWN/LONGTIME MEN'S BASKETBALL COACH, LOUISIANA STATE UNIVERSITY

If you are interested in being an excellent leader, read Pat Williams' latest book, *The Leadership Excellence Devotional*. Pat includes anecdotes and principles you can apply in your everyday life to get the best out of yourself and others. No matter how old you are or what you do in life, this book will help you grow as a person and a leader.

MARK JACKSON/HEAD COACH, GOLDEN STATE WARRIORS

I love this book! These short stories are easy to read and very enlightening. I read a lot of books on leadership but this is the most entertaining. The quotes hit home with a clear message as to what life and leadership are all about. I will recommend it to all my friends.

JIM LARRANAGA/HEAD BASKETBALL COACH, UNIVERSITY OF MIAMI

The Leadership Excellence Devotional

The Seven Sides of Leadership in Daily Life

PAT WILLIAMS
WITH JIM DENNEY

BARBOUR
PUBLISHING

Published by Barbour Publishing, Inc., P.O. Box 719, Uhrichsville, Ohio 44683
www.barbourbooks.com

Our mission is to publish and distribute inspirational products offering exceptional value and biblical encouragement to the masses.

Member of the
Evangelical Christian
Publishers Association

Printed in China.

To my twin grandsons,
Teddy and Jack.
May they grow to become
leaders of excellence.

FOREWORD

Once again, a book by Pat Williams that stretches and challenges me. Pat has a unique way of reminding us of things we tend to forget, or sometimes neglect. Those things that can make the difference between good, better, and best. Pat is like cream—he always rises to the top. He refuses to let his readers settle for second-best thinking and leading.

The Leadership Excellence Devotional: The Seven Sides of Leadership in Daily Life is a valuable book to add to your library. Pat systemizes a lifetime of leadership lessons, allowing us to glean nuggets of wisdom from one of the greatest leaders and motivators I know. These seven sides of leadership are essentials for any leader.

The truths contained here are game-changers. In a world looking for easy answers and a quick climb up the ladder of success, Pat gives us the long upward view. These truths are clearly and concisely laid out. This is the kind of book we need in the fast-paced world in which we live. It's a book for people on the go, who need to slow down and think through how they are leading. It's a book for people wanting to go to the next level, to make sure they are climbing the right ladder. It's a book for seasoned leaders who can easily forget foundational principles while looking for the next new thing.

The powerful quotes and stories in this book will be used over and over again. I plan to purchase multiple copies for up and coming leaders as well as copies for all our staff. We all can use the legacy lessons Pat gives us in this amazingly simple, yet profound book.

MICHAEL CATT
SR. PASTOR, SHERWOOD CHURCH, ALBANY, GEORGIA
EXECUTIVE PRODUCER, SHERWOOD PICTURES

INTRODUCTION

Building a Leadership Legacy, Day by Day

At age seven, I knew I wanted to be a baseball player. I spent countless hours at Shibe Park, cheering for Philadelphia's two major league teams, the Phillies and the A's. While studying the intricacies of the game, I became aware at an early age of the importance of leadership—the role of the catcher as an on-field player-coach, the leadership roles of the manager and base coaches, the executive leadership of the general manager and the owner.

My closest boyhood friend was Ruly Carpenter, whose father, Bob Carpenter, Jr., owned the Phillies. (In later years, from 1972 to 1981, Ruly himself became principal owner.) My connection to the Carpenter family gave me entrée to the behind-the-scenes world of professional baseball and a deeper understanding of leadership in the sports world.

From my school years through my career as a sports executive, I have lived and breathed leadership. I've become personally acquainted with many of the top leaders in sports, business, entertainment, the military, government, and religion.

When I moved to Florida to begin building the dream called the Orlando Magic, the issue of leadership took on a whole new depth of meaning—and a

sense of urgency. Many people told me it was impossible to build an NBA expansion team in a town that had no pro sports tradition.

But I remembered that people had told Walt Disney the things he wanted to do were impossible, too—and right here in Orlando were people who had worked alongside Disney as he built Disneyland in the 1950s. So I talked to every top Disney executive in Orlando and gleaned thousands of leadership insights.

As I began speaking and writing on leadership, I systematized all the leadership lessons I had learned over a lifetime. I discovered that the essence of leadership can be divided into seven categories, or sides, of leadership: Vision, Communication, People Skills, Character, Competence, Boldness, A Serving Heart.

Barbour Publishing recently invited me to pour my lifetime of leadership insights into a book called *Leadership Excellence: The Seven Sides of Leadership for the Twenty-first Century*. Then they asked me to write the book you hold in your hands, *The Leadership Excellence Devotional: The Seven Sides of Leadership in Daily Life*.

One of the serendipitous features of the Seven Sides of Leadership is the number *seven*—the perfect number of principles for a daily study. In the course of a week, you can walk through each of the Seven Sides of Leadership. You can have Vision Sunday, followed by Communication Monday, People Skills Tuesday, Character Wednesday, Competence Thursday, Boldness Friday, and A Serving Heart Saturday.

You can start each day inspired and motivated to reach for the next level of influence as a leader. What better way to build your leadership legacy?

As you live out these leadership principles, I hope you'll call or write me. (My contact information is in the back of the book.) Tell me how these leadership insights are affecting your life and career. I'm eager to hear from you.

God bless you on your leadership journey.

A New Leadership Adventure

Earn your leadership every day.
Michael Jordan

I was exposed to great leaders throughout my early sports career, as both a player and an executive. In 1986, when I arrived in Orlando to build an NBA expansion team from the ground up, I committed myself to an intensive study of leadership principles. Being in Orlando, I also got to explore the leadership traditions of the Walt Disney Company.

In the course of my research, I realized all of the precepts of leadership excellence could be distilled into seven principles I call the Seven Sides of Leadership. These principles are ageless and universal. They were true in the golden age of King Solomon, and they are still true in the Internet Age. These seven principles have been proven by great generals from Alexander the Great to Norman Schwarzkopf, great business leaders such as Steve Jobs and Jeff Bezos, and great religious leaders like Billy Graham and Pope John Paul II.

As we begin our journey, consider the Seven Sides of Leadership: Vision, Communication, People Skills, Character, Competence, Boldness, and A Serving Heart. Which are you strong in? Which do you need to study and master?

A brand new leadership adventure begins for you—*right now.*

Moses said to the Lord, "May the Lord, the God who gives breath to all living things, appoint someone over this community to go out and come in before them, one who will lead them out and bring them in, so the Lord's people will not be like sheep without a shepherd."
Numbers 27:15–17

Seven Sides in Perfect Balance

Leading like Jesus is not a technique. It is a transformation of the heart.
JAMES W. RUEB

Jesus was the greatest leader who ever lived.

Hitler and Stalin were "great" only in the annals of mass murder. Cyrus the Great and Alexander the Great each conquered the known world of his time—but both empires crumbled to dust. Jesus was great because He was totally good and because His kingdom continued to expand even after He left the world.

Jesus exhibited all Seven Sides of Leadership in perfect balance. He was a leader of *Vision*—His vision was "the kingdom of heaven."

He was a master of *Communication*. He attracted crowds and taught deep truth through simple stories. His Sermon on the Mount is the greatest speech ever delivered.

Jesus was adept at *People Skills*. He empathized with people, loved them, and always gave them exactly what they needed. He perfectly epitomized *Character* and every moral virtue.

Jesus personified *Competence*. No one ever taught, trained, delegated, or led as competently as He did. He exemplified *Boldness* when debating His opponents, proclaiming His vision, and enduring the cross.

Above all, Jesus demonstrated *A Serving Heart*. He modeled servanthood when He washed the disciples' feet—and when He hung on the cross. The more completely we build the Seven Sides of Leadership into our lives, the more Christlike we will be as leaders.

> *"Whoever serves me must follow me; and where I am, my servant also will be. My Father will honor the one who serves me."*
>
> JOHN 12:26

Who Controls Your Future?

The Bible teaches us to fear not.
That's a good starting point for any aspiring leader.
BOBBY BOWDEN

Former Florida State football coach Bobby Bowden once told me, "In more than fifty years of college coaching, I have held many jobs, but I never applied for one of them. All of my coaching jobs were handed to me as the Lord Jesus Christ led me through my career. All I did was trust Him. He did the rest."

It takes a bold faith to say, "Lord, You are in the driver's seat. Take control of my life. I leave it all in Your hands." As leaders, we tend to define leadership as *being in control*. But Bobby Bowden describes a different kind of leadership that says, "Lord, *You* are in control."

Bowden traces his trusting attitude to the time he was diagnosed with rheumatic fever at age thirteen. He spent six months in the hospital and more than a year confined to his bed at home. He spent many hours listening to the radio, especially Alabama football games on Saturday mornings.

In his book *Called to Coach*, Bowden recalls, "I prayed to God and told Him that if He healed me from rheumatic fever, I would serve Him through football."[1] God answered that prayer, and Bowden kept his promise.

Who controls your future? Who's in the driver's seat of your leadership life?

Trust in the LORD with all your heart and lean not on your own understanding; in all your ways submit to him, and he will make your paths straight.

PROVERBS 3:5–6

Be a Tomorrow Thinker

The only thing worse than being blind is having sight but no vision.
HELEN KELLER

In *Be All You Can Be*, John Maxwell offers this wise insight: "The poorest person in the world is not the person who doesn't have a nickel. The poorest person in the world is the one who doesn't have a vision. If you don't have a dream—a goal and a purpose in life—you're never going to become what you could become.... Successful people are motivated by a dream beyond them. They have a dream that is bigger than themselves; they have something that constantly keeps them going. It's out of their reach, and yet they believe that if they work hard enough, they will someday hold that dream in their hands.... Unsuccessful people are only motivated by today. They are not tomorrow thinkers."[2]

The people John Maxwell calls "tomorrow thinkers" get the most out of every day. By envisioning a bright tomorrow, they motivate themselves for today's challenges. A vision has incredible power to focus our thoughts and harness our energies.

Dreams of tomorrow help us to persevere through adversity, endure criticism, and finish strong. If you want to be a successful leader, post your vision where everyone can see it. Make tomorrow appear so attractive and exciting that people will go through walls to achieve it.

The future belongs to leaders of vision.

And the LORD answered me: "Write the vision;
make it plain on tablets, so he may run who reads it."
HABAKKUK 2:2 ESV

"Everybody Grab an Oar!"

The key to successful leadership today is influence, not authority.
KENNETH BLANCHARD

Tom Kelly managed the Minnesota Twins from 1986 to 2001, leading them to World Series titles in 1987 and 1991. Retired catcher Tim Laudner believes the key to Kelly's leadership success was *communication*. After one disastrous road trip, the players boarded the team bus and the manager got up to address the team.

"Look," Kelly said, "we're all in this thing together. And if you can't find a way to pull for your teammates, then you need to get off this bus. We're going to have twenty-five guys on this ball club rowing the boat. So, everybody grab an oar, because we're all going to row the boat together. We're going to do this thing together, someway, somehow."

That speech, Laudner said, "was *the* defining moment of the season. . . . When we got home we started pulling for each other, and good things started happening."[3]

Former Twins pitcher George Frazier agrees. He recalls that Kelly "didn't say a lot, but when he spoke—it was meaningful." Kelly's "grab an oar" speech pulled the team together and gave the Twins a vision of who they were as a team. "He was the guy steering that boat," Frazier concludes, "and we all just rode along with him—right to the World Series title."[4]

Great leaders invoke memorable word pictures and analogies to teach, inspire, and motivate. How can you improve your communication skills today?

Jesus spoke all these things to the crowd in parables.
MATTHEW 13:34

A Checklist of People Skills

You can always find people with hard skills, but success or failure often depends on the softer people skills. These are more difficult to find.
EVAN M. BERMAN

People skills are sometimes called "soft skills," as opposed to such "hard skills" as technical expertise. People skills have to do with maintaining positive, cooperative relationships with superiors, subordinates, and the public. Good people skills are essential to good leadership. People skills include (but are not limited to):

• *Self-control.* In times of pressure and frustration, leaders with good people skills control their emotions, especially anger. They fix problems, not blame.

• *Even-handedness.* Leaders avoid office politics, factions, and turf wars. They deal with difficult people in a constructive way.

• *Kindness.* Leaders with people skills have compassion and empathy for the feelings of others.

• *Listening skills.* Great leaders care enough to listen and learn.

• *Tolerance and acceptance.* Leaders need to accept different opinions and personality types.

• *Ability to coach and mentor.* Leaders with people skills are committed to their followers' growth as leaders.

• *Unselfishness.* Leaders sacrifice their interests for others.

• *Love.* The ability to love others is the most important people skill of all. Every people skill is an extension of our commitment to love others.

Which people skills do you excel in? Which do you need to strengthen?

Do not seek revenge or bear a grudge against anyone among your people, but love your neighbor as yourself.
LEVITICUS 19:18

The Price of Maintaining Character

Without character, you can't have wisdom, in spite of competence. Without wisdom, you simply can't build and maintain an enduring institution, whether it be a marriage, a family, a team, or a company.

STEPHEN R. COVEY

Bill Lear was an inventor and businessman, best known for founding the Lear Jet Corporation. Soon after the introduction of the Lear business jet in 1963, two of them crashed. When investigators couldn't discover the cause, Lear ordered the grounding of the other fifty-five planes that had been sold—a move that cost him many prospective buyers.

But Lear was committed to doing the right thing at any cost. Not willing to risk the life of a test pilot, he flew one of his own Lear Jets, simulating the conditions under which the planes had crashed. He nearly met the fate of the previous pilots—but he succeeded in isolating and correcting the design flaw. He made the correction in all fifty-five planes at his own expense.

As Dave Kraft concluded in *Leaders Who Last*, it took Bill Lear "two years to rebuild the business. . . . He lost money and risked his own life, but he never compromised his character."[5]

What risks would you take, what price would you pay, to maintain your character?

For this very reason, make every effort to add to your faith goodness; and to goodness, knowledge; and to knowledge, self-control; and to self-control, perseverance; and to perseverance, godliness; and to godliness, mutual affection; and to mutual affection, love.

2 PETER 1:5–7

What It Means to Be Competent

If you don't have time to do it right, when will you have time to do it over?
JOHN WOODEN

Competence is the ability to perform a job properly and effectively; it comes from a combination of personality traits, habits, training, and experience. Competent leaders know themselves well, both their strengths and limitations. They focus on what they do best and delegate the rest. They understand other people and build cooperative relationships. They solve problems and resolve conflict.

As leaders, we should become competent in several dimensions:

Intellectually competent: open-minded and curious, imaginative and creative, always reading, learning, and hungering for knowledge and wisdom.

Courageously competent: bold and decisive, willing to take prudent (not reckless) risks, willing to speak our minds and defend our values; persistent in the face of obstacles and opposition.

Relationally competent: willing to love and forgive others, kind toward everyone without discrimination, and full of empathy and understanding.

Justly competent: fair, impartial, and merciful.

Morally competent: setting an example of humility, self-control, gratitude, a strong work ethic, optimism, and faith in God.

Physically competent: good health, proper exercise and nutrition, and adequate rest so we can lead with energy and vitality.

People who are competent in these dimensions will always be leaders. Which of these competencies are your strengths? Which are your weaknesses?

*Not that we are competent in ourselves to claim anything for ourselves,
but our competence comes from God.*
2 CORINTHIANS 3:5

The Parachuting General

Fortune favors the bold.
VIRGIL

General Matthew Ridgway took charge of the 82nd Airborne Division in August 1942 and oversaw its transition from an infantry unit to a paratrooper unit. Having never jumped out of a plane, Ridgway underwent paratrooper training alongside his men.

He helped plan the D-Day assault on Normandy in June 1944 and bravely parachuted into battle with his troops. Clay Blair, author of *Ridgway's Paratroopers*, writes, "Few American generals in World War II would experience such a hellish nightmare.... [Ridgway] did not yield to pessimism, doubt or fear; or if he did, he gave no outward sign of it."[6]

Where does such boldness come from? Writer Scott S. Smith notes that Ridgway "was fearless in battle in part because of his Christian faith. He felt he would not be killed until the appointed time."[7]

Five years after World War II, the Korean War erupted. When Communist China entered the war, Ridgway took command of the 8th Army. He found brave soldiers facing shortages while well-fed commanders sat comfortably away from the front. Ridgway fired lazy officers and promoted bold officers in their place. In January 1951, Ridgway launched a counteroffensive that saved South Korea from being overrun.

Some historians believe that China planned to attack Japan next. General Ridgway may well have been the one leader who averted World War III. He was laid to rest in 1993 at age ninety-eight—an inspiring role model of bold, courageous leadership.

"Be strong and courageous, because you will lead these people."
JOSHUA 1:6

Embroidered Wisdom

Everybody can be great because anybody can serve.
MARTIN LUTHER KING, JR.

I got to know Coach John Wooden when he was in his nineties. He graciously invited me into his home, where we had many hours of unforgettable conversation. Often, we'd enjoy a meal together at the Valley Inn, his favorite restaurant. Then we'd go back to his condo, and as the Mills Brothers harmonized on his old-fashioned record player, he would recite a poem he had written.

When entering his home, I felt I was in a Hall of Fame lined with photos, plaques, and memorabilia. But the place of prominence in his front hallway was devoted to two people, neither of whom was a sports figure—Abraham Lincoln and Mother Teresa.

"They're my heroes," Wooden once told me. "I admire them for their wonderful character qualities—their courage, selflessness, humility, and the way they served others. Can you think of two better heroes to have than Lincoln and Mother Teresa?"

During one of my visits, I noticed a pillow that adorned the sofa in his den. The pillow had a quotation embroidered on it: "We can do no great things, only small things with great love—Mother Teresa."

That's authentic wisdom from a little woman with a vast heart. As leaders, let's focus on doing everything, including the small things, with great love.

His master replied, "Well done, good and faithful servant!
You have been faithful with a few things; I will put you in charge
of many things. Come and share your master's happiness!"
MATTHEW 25:21

A Life-Giving Vision

Vision is the art of seeing what is invisible to others.
JONATHAN SWIFT

My writing partner, Jim Denney, told me about his life-changing encounter with a Holocaust survivor:

"In the early 1970s, when I was in high school, I heard psychiatrist Viktor Frankl talk about finding meaning in life. Before World War II, Dr. Frankl studied suicidal patients in Vienna. He found that the best therapy for depression was a sense of purpose. From these findings, he developed *logotherapy*, or meaning-centered therapy.

"He had nearly completed his book on logotherapy when the Nazis arrested him, destroyed his manuscript, and sent him to a concentration camp. He knew he would need a reason for living in order to survive the death camps. So he determined to rewrite the destroyed manuscript. While digging trenches, he visualized standing in a warm, brightly lit lecture hall, speaking to an audience about the psychology of meaning and purpose.

"Hearing him say that, I felt my spine tingle. I realized I was there in the warm, brightly lit lecture hall he had imagined. I was actually taking part in the fulfillment of Dr. Frankl's vision.

"That vision helped him survive the Holocaust. He rewrote his book, *Man's Search for Meaning*, and it was published in 1946."

A vision of the future empowers us to overcome the worst life can throw at us and gives us the power to truly *live*. To lead victoriously, be a leader of vision.

Say to them, "The days are near when every vision will be fulfilled."
EZEKIEL 12:23

The Most Powerful Word of All

*Coaches who can outline plays on a blackboard are a dime a dozen.
The ones who win get inside their players and motivate.*
VINCE LOMBARDI

When Vince Lombardi came to Green Bay in 1958, the Packers were the worst team in the NFL. The previous season, Green Bay had lost ten of twelve games, even though five future Hall of Famers played on that team.

Lombardi identified the team's problem as disunity. Players disrespected each other and their coaches. If the Packers were to become great once more, they had to play as a unit. He tried promoting "Packer spirit," but the term was too intangible. Then he started using a new word in team meetings. That word was *love*.

As Lombardi taught his players to love each other, respect each other, and play as one, everything changed. The Packers finished their first season under Lombardi with a winning record, 7–5. Lombardi was named NFL Coach of the Year.

In his second year, the Packers won the NFL Western Conference, and the fans nicknamed him The Pope.

The Packers capped Lombardi's third year with an NFL championship, a 37–0 blowout of the New York Giants. At a dinner in his honor, an emotional Lombardi said, "You've got to care for one another, you've got to love each other, then you know you've got a team."

Leaders unify their teams through the power of their words. And the most powerful word of all is *love*.

*"By this everyone will know that you are my disciples,
if you love one another."*
JOHN 13:35

Leadership and the Golden Rule

We might come closer to balancing the [federal] budget if all of us
lived closer to the Commandments and the Golden Rule.
RONALD REAGAN

James Cash Penney, founder of the JC Penney department store empire, once said, "The Golden Rule finds no limit of application in business." Texas entrepreneur Bill Byrd agrees. He has started up a wide range of organizations, from restaurants to Christian ministries. In his book *Sweet Success*, Byrd recommends the Golden Rule as a sound business precept.

Byrd writes that, as a leader, "you've got a million and one things with which to be concerned.... If you don't keep your focus on your people, you will find it easy to start thinking of them as numbers, as units of production.... That attitude will begin to show in your words, tone, and actions. The result will be discouraged, dispirited, and disloyal employees.

"The mind-set I'm advocating is simply the well-known Golden Rule: Treat others, including your staff, the way you want to be treated yourself. That means showing respect and concern for the people, not just their productivity, and standing by them in tough times...in a word, *love*.

"The flip side of the Golden Rule is that your team will treat you the way you treat them."[8]

Leadership is love. If your people know you love them, they'll go through walls for you. So love your people as you would have them love you.

"Do to others as you would have them do to you."
LUKE 6:31

To Understand Yourself, Practice Integrity

Integrity is built by defeating the temptation to be dishonest.
RICK WARREN

In an interview with the *New York Times*, James Hackett, CEO of the Steelcase furniture company, said that great leaders possess a sense of self-awareness and self-understanding that comes from *integrity*. "That's what people look for and respect and want to follow," Hackett said, adding that his predecessor, Bob Pew, once told him, "If you want to lead others, you've got to have their trust, and you can't have their trust without integrity."

Hackett also learned integrity while playing for legendary Michigan football coach Bo Schembechler. He recalls a story Schembechler told about his dad taking the fireman's exam. Bo's father lost the job to a man who cheated. Young Bo asked, "Why didn't you tell them the other guy cheated?" His father replied, "It wasn't my job to tell them." So Bo asked, "Why didn't *you* cheat?" His dad said, "Who wants to win by cheating?" That incident, Hackett concluded, shaped Bo Schembechler's leadership ethic.

Hackett often talks to young people about integrity. "I tell them you almost have to practice for those moments when your integrity might be tested," he says. Imagine yourself in a situation where doing the right thing could get you fired. No one would know if you did wrong. Practice making the honest choice, even if you lose your job.[9]

Mental practice conditions you to maintain your integrity in real-life crises. To truly understand yourself, be a leader of integrity

I will conduct the affairs of my house with a blameless heart.
PSALM 101:2

Great Leaders Are Lifelong Learners

Anyone who stops learning is old. . . .
Anyone who keeps learning stays young.
HENRY FORD

Joy Covey was CFO and top strategist at Amazon.com during the online retailer's early hyper-expansion phase in the late 1990s. She left in 2000 with sufficient wealth to focus full-time on family, travel (as a private pilot), and philanthropy.

Covey took an unusual path to leadership. She told an interviewer, "I didn't finish high school—left home when I was fifteen…and worked as a grocery clerk." She completed a four-year college degree in two and a half years, saying, "I wanted to get on with things." She sharpened her thinking skills at Harvard Law School.

Her unorthodox approach to life was an asset in the no-boundaries online commerce world. "I acquired a sense of independence in how I make decisions," she said. "It's really helped me not worry so much whether other people approve of my choices."[10]

After leaving Amazon.com, Covey filled a gap in her education. "Having been fairly utilitarian in the way I went about college," she said, "I didn't have a deep liberal arts background." So she pursued a master's in liberal arts.

Today, Covey dotes on her son, Tyler, pursues outdoor adventures, and works with the Endangered Wolves Center, helping to bring back wild Mexican gray wolves (there are only fifty in the wild).[11]

Who would imagine that a high school dropout would become a lifelong learner and achieve so much? Are you a lifelong learner? How far will learning take you?

Let the wise listen and add to their learning.
PROVERBS 1:5

Bold Leaders Aren't Approval Junkies

We're just monkeys wrapped in suits, begging for the approval of others.
JAKE GREEN, IN THE MOVIE *REVOLVER*

In 1914, an Akron, Ohio, teenager named Aiden Wilson Tozer passed a street preacher who said, "If you don't know how to be saved, just call on God!"

Arriving at home, Tozer went to his attic, knelt down, and called upon God. Five years later, he became a pastor, though he had not attended seminary. Over a forty-four-year career as a pastor and author of more than forty books, A. W. Tozer became known as a leader who sought God's approval, not popular praise. He lived simply, never owned a car, and donated his book royalties to charity.

In *The Price of Neglect*, Tozer writes: "I cannot believe in the spirituality of any Christian man who keeps an eye open for the approval of others. . . . We'll never be where we should be in our spiritual lives until we are so devoted to Christ that we ask no other [approval] than His smile. . . . Then we will know true freedom.[12]

That's wise counsel. A leader who is not a people pleaser is immune to manipulation and flattery, can say *no* with conviction, can decide without fear of criticism, and never feels obligated to make excuses. Bold leaders seek the approval of God, not people.

Am I now trying to win the approval of human beings, or of God?
Or am I trying to please people? If I were still trying to please people,
I would not be a servant of Christ.
GALATIANS 1:10

Servant Leaders Take the Heat

Great leaders take the heat and let their players take the bows.
DAVE ANDERSON

In *Confessions of a Baseball Purist*, sportscaster Jon Miller wrote a tribute to Ralph Houk, who managed the Yankees, Tigers, and Red Sox. Houk, a war veteran, brought military discipline to the game, yet he was also a servant to his players.

"It was really ingenious, the way Ralph operated," Miller explains. "After a game, the press would be all over him, asking questions that invited him to point the finger of blame at one of his players." But Ralph Houk always took the blame himself.

Miller recalled a game involving Red Sox catcher Gary Allenson. In the ninth inning of a tie game at Fenway, the bases were loaded. The Sox attempted a pickoff play, but a wild throw by Allenson allowed the runner on third to score and win the game.

Afterward, Houk told reporters, "I ought to be fired for even thinking about calling that play. I owe my guy an apology. I'm the one who told them to do it, and it didn't work out. I ought to be horse-whipped."[13]

But Houk hadn't called that play. Allenson had called it—but Houk took the blame. The players loved him for it, and their love for their leader motivated them to play all the harder. A leader is a servant who lays down his life for his people.

"I am the good shepherd. The good shepherd lays down his life for the sheep."
JOHN 10:11

Great Leaders Embrace Change

You think there's a line of sight, and then it's gone.
There's suddenly a new angle. . . . We need to systematize change.
BETH COMSTOCK

Whether you lead in the business arena, the church arena, the government arena, or the sports arena, the pace of change is accelerating. Leaders who cannot adapt to change will be steamrolled by it.

As Robert Safian observes in *Fast Company* magazine, the smartphone market in 2007 was dominated by three companies: Nokia, Research in Motion, and Motorola. Within five years, that multibillion-dollar industry had been upended, leaving Apple and Samsung in command.

Across the leadership landscape, long-established ways of doing things are being radically redefined. Automobiles, Safian notes, have become "rolling, talking, cloud-connected media hubs."[14] Social media, such as Twitter, has affected everything from marketing to politics to practicing our faith. Leaders who ignore change risk extinction.

At Creation, God's Spirit moved over the waters, preparing to initiate change in the universe. That same dynamic Spirit moves in our lives today, producing (as Paul writes) "the new creation. . . . The old has gone, the new is here!" (2 Corinthians 5:17).

To embrace God is to embrace change. God does not operate by a predictable paradigm. He works through flux and chaos—and so should we. When crises come, don't panic—innovate! That's the essence of leadership.

"See, I am doing a new thing! Now it springs up; do you not perceive it?
I am making a way in the wilderness and streams in the wasteland."

ISAIAH 43:19

Great Leaders Are Excellent Listeners

It takes a great man to be a good listener.
CALVIN COOLIDGE

When I was a minor league baseball executive in the 1960s, I had to go to Philadelphia Phillies owner Bob Carpenter and tell him that an individual in the organization was disrupting his business. My stomach was in knots as I entered the executive offices, sat across the table from the owner, and laid it all out.

Then Mr. Carpenter sighed and said, "Why am I always the last to know?"

All too often, leaders find themselves completely in the dark about major problems in their organizations. That's why leaders must be good listeners. They must not only *hear* people out—they must *draw* people out.

The apostle James offers sound leadership advice when he writes, "Be quick to listen, slow to speak, and slow to become angry" (James 1:19). Leaders must continually be aware that followers are reluctant to bring bad news. If you are quick to listen and slow to become angry, your followers will know they can bring you *any* information, good or bad, and you won't "kill the messenger."

Great leaders don't wait for information to come to them. They seek it out. General George Patton said that leaders should always talk to the soldiers. The troops, he said, "know more about the war than anybody. Make them tell you all of their gripes. Make sure they know we are doing everything we can to help them."[15]

When there's bad news in your organization, make sure you're not the last to know.

To answer before listening—that is folly and shame.
PROVERBS 18:13

Love Your Neighbor as Yourself

A true leader has the confidence to stand alone, the courage to make tough decisions, and the compassion to listen to the needs of others.
Douglas MacArthur

Senator Sam Brownback of Kansas once spent twelve hours in the Ellsworth Correctional Facility. He ate and talked with the prisoners and spent the night locked up in a cell. It wasn't his first visit to Ellsworth, nor his last. He spent the night there as a sign of identification with the men behind bars.

Senator Brownback defies ideological labels. He calls for limited government and lower taxes, yet speaks of reaching out to "the poor and dispossessed." He is deeply concerned for the unborn, the disabled, and poor immigrants—documented or not.

He has a special concern for Africa and has sponsored legislation to deal with ethnic cleansing, slavery, malaria, and AIDS. *The Weekly Standard* said of him, "Arguably no senator has done more to press for human rights and democracy, or to confront the spread of deadly disease."

A plaque on his office wall reads, "Love Your Neighbor as Yourself." He's known for working well with political opponents. Former senator Jim DeMint said, "I'd be surprised if he's said a negative word about anyone."[16]

Senator Brownback leads from heartfelt faith and compassion. What are you doing today to set a compassionate leadership example?

This is what the Lord Almighty said: "Administer true justice; show mercy and compassion to one another. Do not oppress the widow or the fatherless, the foreigner or the poor. Do not plot evil against each other."
Zechariah 7:9–10

Hero—or Antihero?

Integrity is telling myself the truth.
And honesty is telling the truth to other people.
SPENCER JOHNSON

I extolled cyclist Lance Armstrong as a role model in books and speeches. I considered him a hero. I was fooled.

USA Today's Christine Brennan named Armstrong "2012's anti-sportsman of the year, hands down. He lied, cheated, bullied, and deceived his way to seven Tour de France titles and millions of dollars from those who believed his story was pure and true. It wasn't. Not even close."[17] His deception is all the more offensive, Brennan writes, because Armstrong set himself up as "far more than a superb athlete. He had marketed himself as a superb person, too."[18]

In 1996, at age twenty-five, Armstrong was diagnosed with advanced testicular cancer that had spread to his lungs and brain. Though doctors gave him slim hope of survival, surgery and chemotherapy saved his life. Beating cancer became part of the Lance Armstrong legend.

Allegations of doping dogged him, though he had passed some six hundred drug tests. Armstrong called himself "the most tested athlete in the world." But in 2012, the United States Anti-Doping Agency released evidence that Armstrong had operated "the most sophisticated, professionalized and successful doping program that sport has ever seen."[19]

In a January 2013 interview with Oprah Winfrey, Armstrong finally confessed. Now he's stripped of his titles and hero image and being sued for millions. The next time you're tempted to betray your integrity, remember antihero Lance Armstrong.

Whoever walks in integrity walks securely,
but whoever takes crooked paths will be found out.
PROVERBS 10:9

Investor's Business Daily's
Ten Success Secrets

Every action and feeling is preceded by a thought.
JAMES ALLEN, *AS A MAN THINKETH*

Over the years, *Investor's Business Daily* has made an intensive study of successful leaders from many fields of endeavor. From that study, the *IBD* editors distilled ten traits that all successful people have in common. They are (in slightly condensed form) as follows:

1. *How you think is everything.* Be positive and focus on success, not failure.
2. *Decide on your true dreams and goals.* Write down your goals, and have a written plan for achieving them.
3. *Take action.* Dreams minus action equals daydreams. Just do it.
4. *Never stop learning.* Keep reading, studying, training, and learning.
5. *Be persistent and work hard.* Refuse to give up.
6. *Learn to analyze details.* To make good decisions, get all the facts.
7. *Focus your time and money.* Don't let people pull you off course.
8. *Don't be afraid to innovate.* Dare to be different.
9. *Deal with people effectively.* Practice communication and people skills.
10. *Be honest and dependable.* If you aren't, traits 1–9 won't matter.[20]

Great leaders are positive, focused, goal-oriented people who think clearly, act boldly, speak honestly, and never give up. Build these habits of thinking and acting into your daily leadership life and you can't help but succeed.

For as he thinks within himself, so he is.
PROVERBS 23:7 NASB

"God Is the Source . . ."

We need to be visionary; we have to be bold.
ANGELA HUNT

From 1974 through 1986, I coordinated and emceed the Sunday morning chapel services for the Philadelphia Phillies. When I left in June 1986 to move to Orlando, the players presented me with a study Bible. They all signed the frontispiece, and Hall of Fame third baseman Mike Schmidt added a personal note:

Pat, I am a better man for having known you.
Thanks for your influence in my life.
God bless you. Mike Schmidt.

Mike has no greater admirer in the world than yours truly. My third son, Michael Patrick Williams, is named after him.

Widely considered the greatest third baseman in history, Mike played his entire career with the Phillies. He earned ten Gold Glove Awards, nine of them consecutive. He holds team records in games played, home runs (548), runs scored, hits, RBIs, and on and on.

In 1990, the Phillies retired Mike's number 20. At his Tribute Night speech, he said, "I'd like to talk about my faith. . . . God is the source for all my strength, physical and mental. In 1977, God entered my life. My faith in Him provided a foundation for my life and my career."

I admire the boldness of Mike Schmidt. When the fans gathered to pay tribute to Mike, he pointed heavenward and paid tribute to God. His example inspires us as leaders to boldly proclaim our faith in God as the source of our strength and our success.

[Paul] proclaimed the kingdom of God. . .with all boldness.
ACTS 28:31

A Leader Who Seeks God's Pleasures

Life! Joy! Pleasures! Who enjoys these priceless blessings? Those who walk on God's path, live in God's presence, and seek God's pleasures.
WARREN WIERSBE

In fall 2012, I visited Dr. Warren Wiersbe at his Lincoln, Nebraska, home. A renowned leader and the author of 160 books, Dr. Wiersbe was my pastor in Chicago when I was general manager of the Bulls from 1971 to 1973.

Dr. Wiersbe took me to his basement—and I gasped! His basement is a vast library of around ten thousand books. Running the length of his house, it is organized by sections: history, theology, psychology, and so forth.

He signed several of his own books for me with the reference "Psalm 16:11." As a young man at seminary in Chicago in 1948, he asked God for a verse of reassurance for difficult times, and God gave him that verse.

Over lunch, I asked Dr. Wiersbe his philosophy of leadership. He said, "My philosophy is simple: Leaders are people with all the weaknesses of everyone else. They use their God-given talents to lead and train others to lead. They use every opportunity to bring God-given character qualities out of others so they can become leaders, too." In short, *the job of a leader is to build more leaders.*

That's the kind of leader Dr. Wiersbe has been, and the kind I want to be.

You make known to me the path of life; you will fill me with joy in your presence, with eternal pleasures at your right hand.
PSALM 16:11

A Vision for the Next Generation

Leadership is the capacity to translate vision into reality.
WARREN G. BENNIS

Oprah Winfrey is a woman with a vision for lifting children out of poverty. She once mentored girls from inner-city Chicago, taking them on outdoor adventures, introducing them to great books, and more. But when the girls returned home, family members mistreated them out of envy. Oprah concluded, "You can't just give people money, new homes, new stuff, and think that you're giving them a new life."

That failed experiment led Oprah to direct her compassion toward South Africa, where she founded the Oprah Winfrey Leadership Academy for Girls. Though the academy had its problems and controversies, Oprah persevered. Concerned about "a lack of leadership on all levels" in the world, Oprah wants the girls at the academy to "understand their own power and possibility."[21]

She gets emotional talking about her students, such as the girl who lost four close relatives to AIDS in one year. Yet she also demands that the girls respect the privilege of attending the academy. When Oprah learned that some were slacking off in their studies, she confronted them.

"Everybody talks about unconditional love," she told the girls. "My love has some conditions.... I've given you my best, and that's what I want from you. I want your best." The girls got the message.[22]

Oprah Winfrey is a leader with a vision for the next generation. What is *your* leadership vision?

May he give you the desire of your heart and make all your plans succeed.
PSALM 20:4

The Willingness to Confront

When you confront a problem, you begin to solve it.
RUDY GIULIANI

Sometimes leaders need to confront. And sometimes leaders need to be confronted. In 2 Samuel 11–12, we see both principles in operation. We see a prophet with the courage to confront his king.

It's the story of King David and Bathsheba. David committed adultery with Bathsheba, resulting in her pregnancy. Then he covered up his sin by arranging for the murder of Bathsheba's husband, Uriah the Hittite.

So God sent the prophet Nathan to King David to confront him. Nathan began by telling the king a story about a rich man who cheated a poor man, taking away the poor man's only possession, a beloved ewe lamb. Hearing the story, King David said that the rich oppressor deserved death.

Then Nathan said, "You are the man! . . . Why did you despise the word of the LORD by doing what is evil in his eyes?" (2 Samuel 12:7, 9).

To paraphrase Shakespeare's *Hamlet*, the story of the lamb was the thing with which to catch the conscience of the king. Nathan used all of his communication skills to reach David's conscience—drama, suspense, surprise, and direct confrontation.

King David responded with genuine remorse: "I have sinned against the LORD" (2 Samuel 12:13). He later composed Psalm 51, a psalm of confession and repentance.

Sometimes we are called to confront others—including other leaders. It takes courage, wisdom, and communication skills to reach another person's conscience. What have you done today to improve your communication skills?

Jesus called the crowd to him and said, "Listen and understand."
MATTHEW 15:10

A Great Love for People

In order to lead people, you must love people.
ROY E. ALSTON

In 1930, New York Giants founder Timothy Mara divided ownership of the team between his two sons, twenty-two-year-old Jack and fourteen-year-old Wellington. At age twenty, in 1936, Wellington became a key figure in the first NFL draft. Back then, teams had no scouts, so team executives had little to go on when drafting players. Yet Wellington Mara displayed amazing insight into college football talent.

In that first draft, Mara advised the Giants to take Alphonse "Tuffy" Leemans, a George Washington University running back. Leemans went on to a Hall of Fame career, which included winning an NFL championship in 1938.

Mara's intense interest in people gave him an edge in recruitment. How did he know Leemans would be a star? He had subscribed to hundreds of newspapers and compiled dossiers on many college players. After following Leemans's GWU career, Mara attended a game and saw a spectacular Leemans performance.

Wellington Mara's players loved him because he loved them. Linebacker Harry Carson said, "The Giants' organization cares about its players more than most teams.... Wellington, especially, has sought to cultivate a family atmosphere." Linebacker Lawrence Taylor said, "Nobody did more for me than Wellington Mara."[23]

In 2005, as Wellington Mara lay dying at age eighty-nine, his players dedicated a game to their beloved owner—then shut out the Redskins 36–0.[24] Great leaders achieve great goals through their great love for people.

"I am the good shepherd; I know my sheep and my sheep know me."
JOHN 10:14

CEO—Chief Example Officer

Example is leadership.
Albert Schweitzer

In May 2007, the CEO of a major entertainment company resigned following his arrest for allegedly assaulting his girlfriend. The incident prompted the *San Francisco Business Times* to conduct a reader poll with the question, "Should company officers be fired or forced to resign because of personal behavior?"

The results of the poll: Yes: 70 percent. No: about 14 percent. Undecided: about 17 percent.

Readers also offered their opinions on the subject. Here's a sampling of their views: "A leader in business is a leader in life." "Boorish, violent, slanderous, or unprofessional behavior damages a company's brand." "Personal behavior is oftentimes a reflection of one's leadership abilities and shortcomings." "A company's CEO and officers are public figures and should be subject to higher scrutiny."[25]

An article at the ManageBetter.biz website encourages us as leaders to give ourselves a promotion to "CEO"—Chief Example Officer. "Though we usually think of 'setting an example' as something we do unconsciously in the course of the day," the writer observes, "it can also be a planned management technique."[26]

As leaders, we should exemplify the kind of behavior we want our followers to emulate: courtesy, generosity, integrity, hard work, fairness, and sharing information and ideas. If we set a goal of leading by example every day, our followers will notice—and they will follow our lead.

Don't let anyone look down on you because you are young, but set an example for the believers in speech, in conduct, in love, in faith, and in purity.
1 Timothy 4:12

Live and Learn

Self-education is, I firmly believe, the only kind of education there is.
ISAAC ASIMOV

While researching the early lives of business leaders, Adelia Cellini Linecker made a fascinating discovery. She found that Amazon.com founder Jeff Bezos, Wikipedia founder Jimmy Wales, and Google cofounders Larry Page and Sergey Brin all had one thing in common: They had spent their formative years in Montessori schools.

Montessori is a private educational approach based on the theories of Italian physician Maria Montessori. This approach holds that learning is most effective when learners are free to explore and express their creativity.

Is it too late for you and me to learn and become more creative? Absolutely not! Linecker interviewed engineering professor Bhaskar Krishnamachari of the University of Southern California, who said that people of any age can learn and grow in an atmosphere that encourages childlike play and creative freedom.

In fact, adults can reap huge benefits from lifelong learning. Lifelong learners don't have the pressure of taking (and flunking) tests. Krishnamachari concludes that adults who continue to be lifelong learners are more likely to become "fearless, self-motivated individuals who can make bold and innovative discoveries."[27]

Commit yourself to a lifetime of learning. Be creative and have fun as you learn. Treat learning as play. Remain childlike in your curiosity and love of the adventure of learning. The next big innovation just might have your name on it.

Showing aptitude for every kind of learning, well informed, quick to understand, and qualified to serve. . .
DANIEL 1:4

The Art of the Boldly Biblical Burger

Put a grain of boldness into everything you do.
BALTASAR GRACIÁN

In the mood for gourmet fast food? The place to go is In-N-Out Burger. Tom Hanks has In-N-Out delivered to movie sets. Paris Hilton was driving to In-N-Out when she got her infamous DUI. TV's "French Chef," Julia Child, had In-N-Out burgers delivered during a hospital stay.[28]

The California-based chain, founded in 1948 by Harry and Esther Snyder, maintains a simple philosophy: "Give customers the freshest, highest quality foods you can buy and provide them with friendly service in a sparkling clean environment."[29]

The company pays generous wages, resulting in high employee morale, which is reflected in efficient, cheery service. In-N-Out's great food and immaculate eateries have garnered an intensely faithful following.

In-N-Out is famed for Bible verse references on its packaging, reflecting the Snyder family's Christian values. Burger wrappers feature Revelation 3:20: "Here I am! I stand at the door and knock. If anyone hears my voice and opens the door, I will come in and eat with that person, and they with me." French fry trays feature Proverbs 24:16: "For though the righteous fall seven times, they rise again, but the wicked stumble when calamity strikes." Soda cups display John 3:16 and Double-Double wrappers show Nahum 1:7.

Millions of customers have looked up those verses for a blessing from God's Word. In-N-Out exemplifies the perfect balance of bold business leadership and bold Christian witness. As In-N-Out milkshake cups remind us…

Trust in the LORD with all your heart.
PROVERBS 3:5

Love the People You Don't Like

*I don't necessarily have to like my associates,
but as a man I must love them.*
Vince Lombardi

In 1968, I attended a Fellowship of Christian Athletes summer conference in Black Mountain, North Carolina. I learned that Doug Moe would be there. Doug was a basketball star at the University of North Carolina and later played pro basketball. Because of his maverick reputation, I was surprised he would attend a Christian conference.

I asked conference director Loren Young, "What will you do with Doug Moe?"

Loren replied, "We're going to just love him for a week."

I learned an important leadership lesson from Loren Young: Love is an indispensable part of leadership. The people we lead need our love. The less lovable they are, the more we must love them.

I'm not talking about syrupy-sweet feelings. Leadership love is a function of the will, not the emotions. It's what the Greek New Testament calls *agape* love, and it usually requires that we act in opposition to our feelings.

When we feel angry and frustrated with someone, we need to love that person all the more. *Agape* love says, "I will seek what's best for you, even though, in my emotions, I'd rather deck you."

Anyone can love people they like. It takes character and a serving heart to love people we don't like. That's why leaders are called to serve and to love.

*"If you love those who love you, what credit is that to you?
Even sinners love those who love them."*
Luke 6:32

An Eye on the Future

I wasn't trying to predict the future. I was trying to prevent it.
Ray Bradbury

Yale economist Robert Shiller is an expert in market volatility and the only economist who accurately predicted the stock market bubble of 2000 and the subprime mortgage meltdown of 2008. Shiller credits his father, Benjamin Shiller, for teaching him to think for himself and speak his mind instead of deferring to so-called authorities.

"In 2004, when I wrote the second edition of my book *Irrational Exuberance*," Shiller told *Fortune* magazine, "I was worried that the boom in home prices might collapse, bring on bankruptcy in both households and businesses, and lead to a world recession. I remember thinking that this sounds kind of flaky—nobody else is saying this.... But I had learned from my father not to care what other people think. This was my book, and I believed this, so I just said it."[30]

If only our political and business leaders had listened to Robert Shiller.

Great leaders keep an eye on the future. To become a futurist like Robert Shiller, you must (1) embrace change, (2) inform yourself about trends that will produce change, and (3) learn to plan effectively for change. Make sure you know all the best-case and worst-case scenarios that could affect your organization, and devise strategies that will enable you to thrive in changing times.

Don't let the future take you by surprise.

[Jerusalem] did not consider her future. Her fall was astounding; there was none to comfort her.
Lamentations 1:9

Leaders Must Be Teachers

The best leaders are teachers.
DAVID BARGER

Jack Ramsay (aka Dr. Jack) is a broadcaster and former basketball coach, who led the Portland Trail Blazers to the 1977 NBA championship. He gave me my first job in the NBA. A coach's success, he says, depends on "one's ability to teach his game plan to his staff and players." This is true not only in coaching, but in any leadership arena.

"When I first took over the Trail Blazers," Dr. Jack recalled, "I met with Bill Walton to explain the game I wanted to play and his role in it. He seemed pleased with the theory, and yet I remember his comment as we finished our meeting: 'Coach, one last thing—don't assume we know anything.'"[31] Hearing that Walton and his teammates wanted fundamental teaching, Dr. Jack said he knew they'd have a great team.

Jack Ramsay advocates a "whole-part-whole" teaching method. He explains: "Give the players an overall view of what the end product looks like, break it down into its essential parts, then put all the parts together."[32] Finally, he adds, reinforce verbal and visual teaching through drills and practice.

Even the best players, he adds, "need teaching and are receptive to it." And the best leaders continually do "whatever it takes to teach the game."[33] What will you do today to lead by teaching?

"As for me, far be it from me that I should sin against the LORD by failing to pray for you. And I will teach you the way that is good and right."

1 SAMUEL 12:23

Success Begins with Caring

People don't care how much you know until they know how much you care.
John Maxwell

Indra Nooyi is chairman and CEO of PepsiCo and (according to *Forbes*) one of the world's 100 most powerful women. The married mother of two daughters runs the second-largest beverage company in the world, with almost three hundred thousand employees worldwide.

Succeeding Steven Reinemund as CEO in 2006, Nooyi saw PepsiCo earnings soar under her leadership. Reinemund, now the dean of the Wake Forest University business schools, says Nooyi's people skills give her a decided edge. He calls her "a deeply caring person" who "can relate to people from the boardroom to the front line."

Nooyi was one of two finalists for CEO, and after she got the job, she told the other candidate she wanted to keep him on the PepsiCo team. Though he was disappointed at losing the top job, Nooyi's caring won him over and he stayed on.

Indra Nooyi has steered the company out of the junk food industry and into a more wholesome, health-conscious direction with such acquisitions as Tropicana and Quaker Oats. She has also committed the company to anti-obesity efforts and environmentally conscious policies.

The high-powered exec still makes time for family, phoning her mother in India daily. She reminds herself, "Don't forget you're a mother, don't forget you're a wife, don't forget you're a daughter."[34] These reminders make Indra Nooyi one of America's most caring CEOs.

How do you show you care about the people you lead?

Jesus called his disciples to him and said, "I have compassion for these people."
Matthew 15:32

Set an Example of Self-Discipline

*We are the biggest obstacles to our own happiness. It is much easier to do
battle with society and with others than to fight our own nature.*
DENNIS PRAGER

Former NBA coach Phil Jackson learned self-discipline while a senior at the
University of North Dakota.

"I was captain of the basketball team," he told me, "and we were playing in
Chicago. I went out with friends to Rush Street, and I got back to the hotel after curfew. So Coach Bill Fitch took away my captaincy. He said, 'You won't be
captain again until you prove you deserve it.' Bill made me prove I had the self-
discipline to be captain. In time, I earned my job back. Bill gave me a lesson in
discipline that has helped me throughout my life."

NFL coach Mike Shanahan draws a distinction between external discipline
and self-discipline. "Discipline," he says, "is listening to people tell you what to do,
where to be, and how to do something. Self-discipline is knowing that you are
responsible for everything that happens in your life; you are the only one who can
take yourself to the desired heights."[35]

The Chinese philosopher Laozi said, "He who controls others may be powerful, but he who has mastered himself is mightier still." And King Solomon
writes, "Like a city whose walls are broken through is a person who lacks self-
control" (Proverbs 25:28).

Great leaders set a daily example of self-discipline.

*For the Spirit God gave us does not make us timid,
but gives us power, love and self-discipline.*
2 TIMOTHY 1:7

The Intelligent Christian Leader

The true sign of intelligence is not knowledge, but imagination.
Albert Einstein

British philosopher Bertrand Russell viewed Christianity as an anti-intellectual religion. He writes, "So far as I can remember, there is not one word in the Gospels in praise of intelligence."[36] He could not have been more wrong.

Jesus, in His parables, often contrasted wisdom versus foolishness: the wise and foolish house builders (Matthew 7, Luke 6), the wise and foolish maidens (Matthew 25), and the wise and foolish managers (Luke 12).

When Jesus spoke, people marveled at His intellect. At age twelve, He sat among the teachers in the temple and they were "amazed at his understanding and his answers" (Luke 2:47). As an adult, He debated the teachers, and they said, "How did this man get such learning without having been taught?" (John 7:15; cf. Matthew 13:54). Jesus promised His followers, "I will give you words and wisdom that none of your adversaries will be able to resist or contradict" (Luke 21:15).

In the Old Testament, King Solomon writes, "Let the wise listen and add to their learning" (Proverbs 1:5). God gave the prophet Daniel and his friends "understanding of all kinds of literature and learning" (Daniel 1:17).

The gospel is so simple a child can understand it, yet so deep it challenges the intellect. As a leader, seek wisdom and understanding. God gave you a magnificent mind, and He's pleased whenever you use it to lead others and serve Him.

Instruct the wise and they will be wiser still;
teach the righteous and they will add to their learning.
Proverbs 9:9

Take a Risk for What's Right

I learned that courage was not the absence of fear, but the triumph over it. The brave man is not he who does not feel afraid, but he who conquers that fear.
NELSON MANDELA

On February 1, 1960, four black college freshmen walked into the Woolworth's department store in Greensboro, North Carolina, sat at the "whites only" lunch counter, and waited to be served. Their names: Joseph McNeil, Franklin McCain, Ezell Blair Jr., and David Richmond. The server behind the counter saw them—and ignored them.

A few seats away, a white woman sipped coffee—and watched. Finally, she got up, walked over to the students, and said, "I am so proud of you. Good luck!" Then she left. Encouraged by her words, the four students continued waiting until closing time, then left.

They returned the next day with fifteen more students. The day after that, three hundred students. Then a thousand.

Their silent protest became known as a "sit-in." Within weeks, sit-in demonstrations had spread to other states. Within six months, the Greensboro lunch counter was desegregated. Four years later, President Lyndon Johnson signed the Civil Rights Act into law.

It took courage to do what those four young leaders did. They had warned their families that they expected violence—but they were ready to pay that price for the sake of justice.[37]

As a bold leader, what risks are you willing to take, what price are you willing to pay, for the sake of righteousness and justice?

Be on your guard; stand firm in the faith; be courageous; be strong.
1 CORINTHIANS 16:13

Seven Rules for Successful Servanthood

Good leaders must first become good servants.
ROBERT GREENLEAF

Flavio Martins, vice president of customer support at WinTheCustomer.com, analyzed the leadership style of Sir Richard Branson, founder of the Virgin Group. In his study, Martins identifies what he calls "Richard Branson's Seven Customer Service Success Rules."[38] These are excellent rules for serving in every arena of life:

Rule No. 1: *Saying "Yes!" Is Fun*. Martins says that Branson became successful by saying yes to new ideas and new opportunities. Leaders look for ways to say yes.

Rule No. 2: *Dream Big!* Why merely offer decent service and adequate value when you can *wow* people with your incredible, amazing, unexpected service and value?

Rule No. 3: *Have Fun Serving*. Work hard, work smart, but above all, have fun while you serve others. Deliver service with enthusiasm.

Rule No. 4: *Take Risks!* Don't play it safe. Be bold, be a visionary!

Rule No. 5: *Live for Each Service Moment*. Look for ways to connect with people, to learn their needs, and to meet that need with a serving heart.

Rule No. 6: *Always Give Respect*. Anyone you serve might be in a position to help you someday. Give respect and build a good reputation.

Rule No. 7: *Give Back Through Service*. Money is important, but satisfaction doesn't come from money. It comes from serving others.

Do you want a serving heart? These seven rules are a great place to begin.

"But I am among you as one who serves."
LUKE 22:27

Abraham Lincoln and the Power of Vision

Lincoln's presidency is a big, well-lit classroom for business leaders seeking to build successful, enduring organizations.
HOWARD SCHULTZ

In the last line of his Gettysburg Address, Abraham Lincoln expressed his vision for America: "That this nation, under God, shall have a new birth of freedom—and that government of the people, by the people, for the people, shall not perish from the earth."

Howard Schultz, CEO of Starbucks, says that Lincoln was a visionary leader who "always looked upward and always called American citizens to a higher road and to a purpose bigger than themselves."[39]

Leadership experts George Manning and Kent Curtis write that Lincoln exemplified "the power of vision." They explain, "With compassion for all people and dedication to preserving the Union, Lincoln delivered the Gettysburg address, considered by historians the most powerful speech since the Sermon on the Mount. In so doing, Lincoln articulated a vision of a united America that would inspire and sustain his country through bitter civil war."[40]

Lincoln faced continual opposition and battlefield setbacks during the Civil War. Strategic consultant Ari Bloom says Lincoln's vision guided him through the turmoil of the war: "Some of his ability to navigate such difficult terrain was about emotional intelligence and the deep faith he nurtured about his vision."[41]

Whether you lead a government, a corporation, a team, or a church, your vision of the future will guide you through any leadership terrain.

I remain confident of this: I will see the goodness of the LORD in the land of the living.
PSALM 27:13

Live Well, Speak Well, and Lead

Speech is power: speech is to persuade, to convert, to compel.
RALPH WALDO EMERSON

In late 1996, I had dinner with George McGovern, the South Dakota senator who lost a presidential bid in 1972. He was engaging, yet self-effacing, and he shared many stories about his years in politics.

When I asked about his service in World War II, he said very little. Only later did I learn that, as a B-24 bomber pilot, he flew thirty-five combat missions.

On his final mission, over Austria, McGovern's plane survived a flak barrage that riddled the fuselage and wings with holes. The waist gunner was critically wounded, and the plane's hydraulics and engine were shot away. McGovern had to invent a new way to land the plane, deploying parachutes from the tail to compensate for the lack of flaps. The plane ended up in a ditch, destroyed—but every man survived.

In 2007, I interviewed McGovern about leadership. He told me he had debated in high school and won a statewide speaking contest. These experiences had taught him the value of public speaking as a leadership skill.

He said, "I tell young people, 'Become a good person first, then a good speaker. Use your ability to help others be better people. The life well lived is its own reward.'" Those are wise words from a leader who lived well, spoke well, and served honorably.

> *"Moses was educated in all the wisdom of the Egyptians and was powerful in speech and action."*
> ACTS 7:22

The Dean of Caring Leadership

Honesty, integrity, discipline administered fairly, not playing favorites, recruiting the right people, effective practice and training, and caring are foundations that any organization would be wise to have in place.

DEAN SMITH

Dean Smith coached basketball at the University of North Carolina at Chapel Hill from 1961 to 1997. He retired with 879 victories and two NCAA championships, having won 78 percent of his games.

Famed for leading a clean program with a high graduation rate (96.6 percent), Smith led the desegregation of the university's sports program. An admirer of Dr. Martin Luther King Jr., Coach Smith recruited UNC's first black scholarship player.

Smith once observed, "The most important thing in good leadership is truly caring. The best leaders in any profession care about the people they lead."

Lakers forward Antawn Jamison played for the UNC Tar Heels in the late 1990s. He says that Dean Smith "cared about his players. Not just how they performed on the basketball court, but how they performed in life."

Smith coached Hall of Famers Michael Jordan, James Worthy, and Billy Cunningham, who recalled, "[Smith] knew if Michael Jordan stayed another year he probably would have coached another national championship team, but Dean knew it was the right time for Michael to go pro."[42]

Coach Dean Smith exemplified great leadership through caring about his people. How do you demonstrate caring for the people you lead?

> *"The one who enters by the gate is the shepherd of the sheep. . . . He calls his own sheep by name and leads them out."*
>
> JOHN 10:2–3

Honesty with Oomph

The foundation stones for a balanced success are honesty,
character, integrity, faith, love, and loyalty.
ZIG ZIGLAR

In February 2006, my son Bobby and I went to Houston for the NBA All-Star weekend. Our first day, while we were jogging near our hotel, I saw someone I recognized from TV news reports. "Bobby," I said, "that's Ken Lay."

Lay, the former head of Enron, the collapsed energy company, was on trial for securities fraud. He and his wife were leaving the courthouse and walking toward us. As they approached, I said, "Mr. Lay, I'm Pat Williams with the Orlando Magic."

We shook hands, and he introduced his wife, Linda. I said, "I want you to know I'm praying for you."

He seemed surprised. "I appreciate that," he said.

They crossed the street and Bobby and I jogged on. Bobby said, "He seemed like a nice guy." He did indeed—yet he was accused of a multi-billion dollar securities fraud.

A few months later, the jury found Ken Lay guilty—but on July 5, before he could be sentenced, he suffered a fatal heart attack. Ken Lay had been a preacher's son, a Sunday school teacher, a business leader, and a confidant to presidents. Somewhere along the way, he lost his integrity.

I once asked my son Michael to define integrity. "Integrity," he replied, "is honesty with a little oomph." I like that. So put some oomph in your honesty. Never let go of your integrity. Guard it with your life.

May integrity and uprightness protect me, because my hope, LORD, is in you.
PSALM 25:21

Great Leaders Look Ahead

Those who look only to the past or present are certain to miss the future.
JOHN F. KENNEDY

Tom Landry was one of the greatest, most innovative football coaches in the history of the NFL. He invented many of the formations, techniques, and strategies that are standard in the game today. During his twenty-nine-year career with the Dallas Cowboys, he coached his teams to a record twenty consecutive winning seasons (1966–1985), five Super Bowl appearances, and two Super Bowl championships (VI and XII).

Unlike so many volatile, emotional coaches today, Landry appeared cerebral and emotionless on the sidelines, even in highly charged situations. He once explained why he remained cool and calm no matter what was happening on the field.

"I don't see the game the way the fans do," he said. "While the team is running one play, I'm looking ahead, planning the next one."[43]

That's how great leaders think. They have a job to do, and the job is to lead. That means your thoughts must be focused several steps ahead of the thoughts of your followers and your fans. Yes, you are aware of where the ball is now. But you are even *more* aware of where the ball needs to be—and you are focused on how to get it there.

Great leaders look ahead, think ahead, plan ahead. They manage the present by focusing on the future.

"For I know the plans I have for you," declares the LORD, "plans to prosper you and not to harm you, plans to give you hope and a future."
JEREMIAH 29:11

Leadership Is Not a Democracy

*Leadership is not a democracy. My job as the leader
is to seek input, not consensus.*
Harry Kraemer

Northern newspapers criticized General Ulysses S. Grant for the heavy ca-
sualties sustained in the Battle of Shiloh, despite a decisive Union victory.
President Lincoln appreciated Grant's bold leadership, saying, "I can't spare this
man; he fights."

Grant didn't believe in "leadership by committee." He said that a military
commander should "consult his generals freely but informally, get their views and
opinions, and then make up his mind.... There is too much truth in the old adage,
'Councils of war do not fight.'"[44]

A leader's job is to gather facts, make decisions, and make sure those decisions are carried out. Timid leaders try to limit their liability by putting decisions
to a vote. That's not leadership. That's abdication.

Bill Dann, CEO of Professional Growth Systems, tells of a top executive
who was challenged by a subordinate who wanted a vote on company decisions.
The exec replied, "Are you going to be in front of the board when things go bad?
That's why you don't get to make the decision."[45]

If General Grant were a CEO, he wouldn't call a meeting. He'd catch people in
the hallway or visit their cubicles for an informal chat. Then he'd decide—and accept
full responsibility for his decision. Grant knew: Leadership is not a democracy.

"It is God who arms me with strength and keeps my way secure."
2 Samuel 22:33

Never Too Big for Little Jobs

The only way you can serve God is by serving other people.
RICK WARREN

Don Soderquist joined Wal-Mart Stores in 1980, and served in several executive roles. After the death of founder Sam Walton, Don became the "keeper of the culture" of Wal-Mart.

In August 1980, Wal-Mart opened three stores in Huntsville, Alabama, on the same day. At one store, Don and Sam held a ribbon-cutting ceremony—and were instantly besieged by customers. The aisles were clogged and checkout lines were incredibly long.

"Sam jumped in," Soderquist recalled, "and began to bag merchandise. He handed out candy to the kids and did anything he could think of to help the customers." Sam Walton also got on the public address system, thanked the customers for coming, apologized for the delays and long lines, and offered his personal assistance to any customer in need.

Don Soderquist had always considered himself a service-oriented businessman. But when he saw Sam Walton, the company founder, waiting on customers, bagging merchandise, and giving free suckers to children, he realized he still had a lot to learn about customer service—and he wasn't about to be outdone by the boss.

"Sam taught me a valuable lesson that day," Soderquist concluded. "None of us are too good to do the little jobs. In fact, there are no little jobs. If the chairman of the board wasn't too high and mighty to hand out lollipops and bag goods—neither was I."[46]

"Whoever wants to become great among you must be your servant."
MATTHEW 20:26

The Dream of the Father, the Dream of the Son

I have a dream that one day this nation will rise up and live out the true meaning of its creed: "We hold these truths to be self-evident, that all men are created equal."
Martin Luther King, Jr.

My mother, sister, and I were in the crowd outside the Lincoln Memorial on August 28, 1963, when Dr. Martin Luther King, Jr., gave his "I Have a Dream" speech. Though I didn't grasp the historic importance of that speech at the time, my emotions were stirred by Dr. King's vision.

Dr. King's dream was profoundly influenced by his father, the Rev. Martin Luther King, Sr. ("Daddy King"). For four decades, the elder King led Atlanta's Ebenezer Baptist Church. He also headed Atlanta's NAACP chapter. Daddy King taught young Martin to abhor segregation as an irrational evil.

On one occasion, young Martin went with his father to the shoe store. The white salesman said he would wait on them in the back of the store. Daddy King said he was perfectly comfortable in the front of the store. The salesman refused to budge.

Dr. King later recalled, "He took me by the hand and walked out of the store.... I still remember walking down the street beside him as he muttered, 'I don't care how long I have to live with this [segregated] system, I will never accept it.'"[47]

Daddy King helped shape his son's dream of a world beyond racism and segregation. Whose vision are you helping to shape today?

A future awaits those who seek peace.
Psalm 37:37

Be Yourself

Don't emulate anyone else. Don't try to be someone you're not. Just be yourself.
VINCE LOMBARDI

Here's a leadership lesson from the life of Ronald Reagan, also known as The Great Communicator. In *First Mothers*, Bonnie Angelo writes that Reagan's first movie in 1937 was "an infinitely forgettable effort called *Love Is on the Air*." After attending a screening, Reagan's mother, Nelle, declared, "That's my boy!...He's just as natural as can be. He's no Robert Taylor. He's just himself."[48]

Ronald Reagan agreed that the secret of his success could be found in the adage, "Be yourself." After all, Reagan said, an actor knows two key principles: "To be honest in what he's doing and to be in touch with the audience. That's not bad advice for a politician either. My actor's instincts simply told me to speak the truth as I saw it and felt it."[49]

As you lead, don't try to be anyone else. Don't copy anyone else. Just be yourself. Communicate naturally and confidently—and someday they'll call you a great communicator, too.

Then Saul dressed David in his own tunic. He put a coat of armor on him and a bronze helmet on his head. David fastened on his sword over the tunic and tried walking around, because he was not used to them. "I cannot go in these," he said to Saul, "because I am not used to them." So he took them off.

1 SAMUEL 17:38–39

Better Leadership through Chemistry

Good players are worth nothing if you don't have good chemistry.
JOHN BEILEIN

I grew up in Wilmington, Delaware, home of the DuPont chemical company. For decades, DuPont's slogan was "Better Living through Chemistry."

There's another kind of chemistry in organizations. Chemistry is an elusive quality that produces success. It's made up of such factors as personality, character, job skills, communication skills, and people skills.

Chemistry becomes apparent when you see how your people get along together, play off each other, and mesh their differing strengths. Often, synergy happens, and the whole becomes greater than the sum of the parts. At other times, talented, high-achieving people simply can't get along—and negative chemistry results.

Red Auerbach, the late, great Boston Celtics coach, once said, "Talent alone is not enough. They used to tell me you have to use your five best players, but I've found that you win with the five who fit together best." It's true. A less talented team with great chemistry can often beat a mega-talented team with poor chemistry.

The key to chemistry is a balance of complementary personality types. You need some noisy motivators and some strong, silent types. You need natural leaders and unassuming followers. You need a mix of talents and specialties. Promote good communication to build trust. If you find that happy balance, you'll have chemistry—and you'll win.

Just as a body, though one, has many parts, but all its many parts form one body, so it is with Christ.

1 CORINTHIANS 12:12

Blood, Sweat, and Guts

I'm no miracle man. I guarantee nothing but hard work.
BEAR BRYANT

Paul "Bear" Bryant was one of the greatest coaches in college football history. During his quarter-century of coaching the Alabama Crimson Tide, his teams won thirteen conference championships and six national championships. When he retired in 1982, he held the record for most collegiate football wins with 323. He's remembered for his houndstooth hat, his resonant voice, and his intense work ethic.

Coach Bryant posted this question on his office wall: "What have you traded for what God has given you today?" And he hung these words in his home: "Ask God to bless your work. Do not ask Him to do it for you."[50] Bear Bryant was one of the most quotable coaches who ever stalked a sideline. Here are some of his thoughts on work:

"It's not the will to win that matters—everyone has that. It's the will to prepare to win that matters."

"The old lessons (work, self-discipline, sacrifice, teamwork, fighting to achieve) aren't being taught by many people other than football coaches these days.... We better teach these lessons or else the country's future population will be made up of a majority of crooks, drug addicts, or people on relief."

"There's a lot of blood, sweat, and guts between dreams and success."[51]

To be a leader of distinction, preach and exemplify hard work. Be the "Bear" of your organization.

Whatever you do, work at it with all your heart,
as working for the Lord, not for human masters.
COLOSSIANS 3:23

Making Deposits in the Bank of Experience

Time is not the great teacher. Experience is.
LYNSAY SANDS

Chesley B. Sullenberger III—aka "Captain Sully"—is the US Airways pilot who landed his disabled airliner on New York's Hudson River on January 15, 2009. All 155 passengers and crew survived the incident known as "The Miracle on the Hudson."

The "miracle" began 100 seconds into the flight, when the aircraft hit a formation of geese, causing both engines to fail. When air traffic controllers told Captain Sully they had cleared runways at nearby airports, he replied, "We're going to be in the Hudson."

Sullenberger had not experienced an engine failure before—but he was ready. He told an interviewer, "For forty-two years, I've been making small, regular deposits in this bank of experience, education, and training. And on January 15, the balance was sufficient so that I could make a very large withdrawal."[52]

For years, Captain Sully had logged time in the simulator, practicing strategies for responding to every conceivable emergency, including losing both engines and landing on water. He had practiced that scenario many times—so he had "experience" doing something he'd never done before.

Leaders are often called to do things they've not done before. That's why great leaders prepare themselves to deal with "unthinkable" and "impossible" situations. So be prepared. Keep making deposits into your bank of experience, because you never know when you'll need to make a very large withdrawal.

[Jesus said:] "Be dressed ready for service and keep your lamps burning."
LUKE 12:35

A Mission to a Soviet Prison Camp

He who allows oppression shares the crime.
DESIDERIUS ERASMUS

In 1991, two American congressmen were permitted to enter Perm Camp 35, a Soviet prison camp in the Ural Mountains. The camp was notorious for its brutal punishment of dissidents. The congressmen, Chris Smith of New Jersey and Frank Wolf of Virginia, wanted to see for themselves. They were accompanied by Charles Colson, founder of Prison Fellowship.

Soviet president Mikhail Gorbachev had said that all political prisoners had been freed under his government, but human rights groups claimed that imprisoned dissidents were still fed only once every other day and faced freezing cold, solitary confinement and other injustices. A *New York Times* journalist who visited Perm said that dissidents were imprisoned "for expressing their opinion or for trying to leave the country, or for doing something that in a normal society would not be considered a crime."[53]

The visit by Colson and the congressmen produced results. As Colson later recalled, "As we interviewed each inmate, a KGB officer stood staring and even tape-recording comments, but the prisoners were not intimidated in the slightest. I spoke out against the monstrous gulag system they had been part of. Not long afterward, Perm 35 was closed."[54]

As leaders, we are called to boldly seek justice for the oppressed. We are called to go into hell itself to set a human soul free. Who have you dared to speak out for today?

"He has sent me to proclaim freedom for the prisoners and recovery of sight for the blind, to set the oppressed free."
LUKE 4:18

"If We Can Reach That Spark..."

We have the honor to teach the next generation of servant leaders. It is our job, duty, and privilege to instill in them the passion to effect change and the empathy to think outside themselves.

GWYNETH ANNE BRONWYNNE JONES

Michael Dukakis was elected governor of Massachusetts in 1974. He inherited record unemployment and deficits, yet he successfully led the state to solvency and was twice reelected by wide margins. Governor Dukakis was nominated for president in 1988, but lost to George H. W. Bush.

I once interviewed Governor Dukakis and he told me he's been fascinated with serving and leadership most of his life. "I ran for president of my third grade class," he said. "I wanted to exercise leadership at a young age, and I received encouragement from my teachers and coaches.

"I'm concerned about our ability to attract young leaders for public service. The political climate often paints a poor image of public service. But young people want their lives to count. If we can reach that spark within them, we can motivate them to a lifetime of service. Leadership is service, and I hope we can inspire a generation of idealistic young leaders to serve their world."

What can you do to reach that spark in a young person today? What can you do to encourage a new generation of servant leaders?

Even when I am old and gray, do not forsake me, my God, till I declare your power to the next generation, your mighty acts to all who are to come.

PSALM 71:18

A New Name, a New Vision

Our goal as leaders and educators is to help young people dream big dreams. Teach them how to remove the limits from their thinking and dare to envision the impossible.
Vincent Mumford

Jesus invested extra time and effort in one disciple—Simon Peter.

Simon was the extrovert—the outspoken disciple. Rabbinical tradition says that the name Simon comes from the Hebrew *shama on*, meaning "He [God] has heard," or from *sham 'in*, meaning "there is sin."

When Jesus looked at Simon, He envisioned Simon's future. In Matthew 16:18, Jesus says, "I tell you that you are Peter." The Aramaic word Jesus used was *Cephas*, meaning "stone." In the Greek New Testament, that word is *Petros*. So Jesus called him "Peter the Rock." He also gave Peter a vision of the future: "On this rock I will build my church."

As you read the Gospels, you see that Peter's personality was more like blowing sand than stable rock. He was impulsive and unreliable. In the hours before Jesus went to the cross, Peter denied Jesus three times.

But Jesus wanted Peter to envision himself as a walking Rock of Gibraltar. Jesus knew that Peter's character flaws could be transformed into leadership strengths. So He gave Peter a new name and a vision to live up to.

Leadership is about change. Those who came to Jesus always went away changed. So let's lead like Jesus. Let's give people an inspiring vision of what they could become.

Jesus said to Simon, "Don't be afraid; from now on you will fish for people."
Luke 5:10

Tony Dungy, Leader and Teacher

Nothing is more contagious than example.
François de La Rochefoucauld

One Sunday morning after church, Lori Farmer, a teacher at Pride Elementary School in Tampa Bay, Florida, found a note on her windshield: "I scraped your car backing in. So sorry. Please call me if we don't see you after church. Tony Dungy."

It was true. Her car had been scraped by *the* Tony Dungy, the former coach of the Super Bowl champion Indianapolis Colts. When Farmer contacted Dungy via the phone number on the note, he offered to pay for the damage. But Farmer's car was already scuffed, and she couldn't find any damage.

Dungy insisted on making amends, so Farmer offered a suggestion—a personal appearance at a school assembly. Dungy agreed, and he came to Pride Elementary and spoke to the students on the importance of education, good character, and reaching for their dreams.

Both of Dungy's parents and his wife were educators, so he knows the importance of teaching. He later said he had a lot of fun at the school and he plans to do it again.[55]

When Dungy retired from coaching, his former colleague Herm Edwards of the Kansas City Chiefs said, "He was always a guy who felt that he was a teacher first and foremost. . . . He was a big proponent of. . .helping the players become better football players and better men."[56]

Great leaders set a great example for their followers and for the next generation.

Follow my example, as I follow the example of Christ.
1 Corinthians 11:1

From the Short List to the Enemies List

The challenge of leadership is to be strong, but not rude; be kind, but not weak; be bold, but not a bully; be thoughtful, but not lazy; be humble, but not timid; be proud, but not arrogant; have humor, but without folly.
JIM ROHN

Mark Hatfield served for three decades as a US senator from Oregon. He was the first prominent Republican to oppose the Vietnam War.

His opposition to war was inspired by personal experience. When Pearl Harbor was attacked, Hatfield left college to enlist. As a young navy officer, Hatfield visited Hiroshima and saw the horrible devastation of the atomic bomb.

Though he was on Richard Nixon's vice presidential short list in 1968, he later ended up on Nixon's secret "enemies list" for opposing the president's policies. But Senator Hatfield never considered Nixon his enemy.

When Nixon resigned the presidency after Watergate, he withdrew to his San Clemente compound in disgrace, receiving visits from only a few family members and friends. As Charles Colson writes in *God and Government*, one of the friends Nixon received was Senator Hatfield.

"Without fanfare," Colson writes, "Mark Hatfield, an evangelical Christian, traveled twice to San Clemente. His reason? Simply, as he told me later, 'to let Mr. Nixon know that someone loved him.'"

Colson notes that Senator Hatfield demonstrated how Christian leaders must "bring the values of the Kingdom of God to bear within the kingdoms of man."[57]

Be devoted to one another in love. Honor one another above yourselves.
ROMANS 12:10

How Will You Face the Storms?

No matter what storms are raging all around,
you'll stand firm if you stand on His love.
CHARLES STANLEY

I'm about two years into my battle with multiple myeloma—cancer of the plasma cells in the bone marrow. The Lord has been teaching me that we all go through storms in our lives. We are either coming out of a storm, in the middle of a storm, or heading into a storm. The question is: *How will we face the storm?*

I've been a Christian for many decades, and I've gone through crises and losses before. But this is the first life-and-death struggle I've experienced. When I received the diagnosis, God had my full attention.

At a time like this, we have a choice to make: We can shake our fist at God, complain about life's unfairness, and ask, "Why me?" Or we can take a flying leap into God's lap, throw our arms around His neck, and cling as tightly as we can while we ride through the storm. I've chosen to put all my trust in Jesus Christ.

There's a storm in your path. It may be raging all around you. How will you face life's storms?

"Therefore everyone who hears these words of mine and puts them into practice is like a wise man who built his house on the rock. The rain came down, the streams rose, and the winds blew and beat against that house; yet it did not fall, because it had its foundation on the rock."
MATTHEW 7:24–25

Pay Your Dues

It is extremely rare to reach the apex of your career in your twenties or thirties. . . . There is a certain amount of information you must absorb, both academically and experientially, before you reach the top. It's called paying your dues.

JAN YAGER

General Colin Powell, former secretary of state, recalled that, as a young infantry officer, he learned a lot of barracks wisdom from army captains who had served in prior wars. One old captain told him the following story:

A brash young second lieutenant was eager for advancement. One night at the officer's club, he saw a grizzled old general sitting at the bar.

"Sir," he said, "how do I become a general?"

"Son," the old general said, "you've got to work like a dog. You've got to have moral and physical courage. . . . You must always be the leader."

"Thank you, sir," the second lieutenant said. "So that's how I become a general!"

"No," the general corrected, "that's how you become a first lieutenant. Then you keep doing it over and over."

Powell concludes, "I've always tried to do my best today, think about tomorrow, and maybe dream a bit about the future. But doing your best in the present has to be the rule. You won't become a general unless you become a good first lieutenant."[58]

That's sound advice in any leadership arena.

Do your best to present yourself to God as one approved, a worker who does not need to be ashamed and who correctly handles the word of truth.

2 TIMOTHY 2:15

The Facets of Boldness

Boldness be my friend.
WILLIAM SHAKESPEARE

Boldness means courage. Leadership boldness is expressed in a number of different ways.

Boldness is the courage to step up. Most people are willing to be led. It takes courage to say, "I'll lead the way."

Boldness is the courage to take a lonely stand. Bold leaders are willing to sacrifice their position, their security, and even their lives to make a principled stand for what is right and true.

Boldness is the courage to take risks. There is no such thing as timid leadership. A leader must be willing to make the tough decisions when the outcome is in doubt.

Boldness is the courage to accept responsibility. Bold leaders accept the blame for their mistakes and for the failures of their team or organization.

Boldness is the courage to face the truth. Insecure and cowardly people avoid facts and opinions that contradict their preconceived notions. Bold leaders invite opposing opinions. They want to know the truth, even at the risk of being proved wrong.

Boldness is the courage to persevere against obstacles and opposition. Quitting is often the easy way out—but quitting is not an option for a bold leader.

Boldness is the courage to remain morally pure in a cynical, corrupt world.

Leaders must be willing to sacrifice, suffer, and endure for the sake of their followers. There can be no leadership without boldness.

For I did not shrink from declaring to you the whole counsel of God.
ACTS 20:27 ESV

"I Love to See Other People Shine"

The servant-leader is servant first.
ROBERT GREENLEAF

Ping Fu is the CEO of Geomagic and sits on the National Advisory Council on Innovation and Entrepreneurship. It's astonishing how far she's come.

She grew up during China's Cultural Revolution. Mao's Red Guard raped, beat, and imprisoned her because her parents were educated. In 1984, twenty-five-year-old Ping Fu reached America with eighty dollars in her pocket. Her book *Bend, Not Break* tells how she went from a poor immigrant worker to a successful entrepreneur.

Her secret: servant leadership. When she started her business, she realized programming wasn't her strong suit, so she assembled a talented team and served them to make them successful.

"Today," she says, "I realize what I did is servant leadership. . . . I love to see other people shine. . . . I want to create an environment where people really love what they do and enjoy working with each other.

"I get so happy and I get chills in my spine when people love working together. I don't want people to even notice I'm there, but notice the environment I'm creating, the work they are doing, and the company."

Leaders, Ping concludes, should not be focused on upward mobility. "Think about moving forward rather than up," she says.[59] In other words, think about being a servant rather than a boss—wise advice from someone who's come a long way and is still moving forward.

> *. . .not lording it over those entrusted to you, but being examples to the flock.*
> 1 PETER 5:3

Truett Cathy's Vision of "Something Special"

*Truett Cathy has the clearest vision on how the store should run. . .
then he depends on us to keep it fresh.*
BUREON LEDBETTER

Founded in 1946 by Truett Cathy, the Chick-fil-A restaurant chain is a unique company with a distinctive vision. The company exists to "glorify God by being a faithful steward of all that is entrusted to us" and to "have a positive influence on all who come in contact with Chick-fil-A."

One way the company fulfills its vision is with its "closed on Sunday" policy. Some experts question Chick-fil-A's practice of remaining closed on Sunday—one of the most profitable days in the restaurant industry.

But Truett Cathy believes this policy tells the world there is "something special" about Chick-fil-A. As a company press release says, "There must be something special about the way Chick-fil-A people view their spiritual life and. . .there must be something special about how Chick-fil-A feels about its people."

The policy makes good business sense. By giving employees a day of rest for family or worship, Chick-fil-A attracts quality employees. Sales figures prove that Chick-fil-A restaurants generate more business per square foot in six days than many competitors produce in seven. "It's the best business decision I ever made," Cathy says.[60]

How does *your* values-based vision affect the way you lead your organization every day?

*"Observe the Sabbath day by keeping it holy,
as the LORD your God has commanded you."*
DEUTERONOMY 5:12

The Leader Who Communicates with God

I have so much to do that I shall have to spend the first three hours in prayer.
MARTIN LUTHER

Thomas Walter "T. W." Wilson was a longtime executive assistant to evangelist Billy Graham. A pastor, speaker, and evangelist in his own right, Wilson gave his life to Christ at the same revival meeting where Billy Graham accepted the Lord. From that day until Wilson's death at age eighty-two, the two remained close friends and partners in ministry.

"Ruth and I have lost one of the closest friends we have ever had," Dr. Graham reflected after Wilson's passing in May 2001. "We prayed, laughed, and wept on hundreds of occasions."

Cliff Barrows, the Graham organization's music director, also reflected on the life and faith of T. W. Wilson. "When T. W. was called upon to pray," Barrows said, "no matter where it was, he would begin with the word *and.* 'And our heavenly Father…' It was as though he were carrying on a conversation with the Lord Jesus, and he was just adding this other petition, or this other statement of love and adoration to his ongoing conversation with the Lord."[61]

T. W. Wilson had an understanding of prayer and a walk with God that all leaders should emulate. He didn't pause occasionally to pray. Instead, as the apostle Paul urges us to do in 1 Thessalonians 5:17, T.W. prayed continually. He prayed without ceasing.

The first obligation of every leader is to communicate daily with God.

*Then Jesus told his disciples a parable to show them
that they should always pray and not give up.*
LUKE 18:1

How to Suffer Fools

We must learn to live together as brothers or perish together as fools.
MARTIN LUTHER KING, JR.

Someone once said, "I don't suffer fools gladly, but I gladly make fools suffer." I personally dislike calling anyone a "fool." Jesus bluntly said, "Anyone who says, 'You fool!' will be in danger of the fire of hell" (Matthew 5:22). And I'm pretty sure you can't get around it by substituting the word *moron* for *fool*.

Jesus "suffered" (put up with) foolish people, including His twelve foolish disciples. And He still suffers foolish people today, if I'm any indication.

Political consultants James Carville and Paul Begala offer this perspective on fools: "Jesus said the poor will always be with us. But He could have said the same thing about fools. . . . As you're reading this, certain people come to mind. They're the fools, and you are the gifted one. But. . .someone else is reading this and thinking about you. . . .

"If your only way to handle people you think are fools is by belittling them, you're going to be awfully lonely. It's easy to berate someone. But it takes an enormous amount of creativity, energy, and leadership to bring someone along with you who perhaps doesn't get it at first. And if you're really good, maybe one day that fool will get it. . . .

"There is simply no way to get by in this world without dealing with fools."[62]

I am obligated both to the Greeks and non-Greeks,
both to the wise and the foolish.

ROMANS 1:14

The "Past Exonerative" Tense

The price of greatness is responsibility.
WINSTON CHURCHILL

One of America's most baffling foreign policy failures was the terrorist attack on the US consulate in Benghazi, Libya, on September 11, 2012. The attack killed Ambassador Chris Stevens and three others. After the attack, we learned that Ambassador Stevens had pleaded with the State Department to beef up security at the consulate—but his pleas were ignored.

In October, Secretary of State Hillary Clinton told CNN, "I take responsibility. I'm in charge of the State Department's sixty thousand-plus people all over the world, 275 posts."[63] Translation: "I accept abstract responsibility, but I'm not to blame. My job is so big that I can't be held personally responsible for anything that happens on my watch."

This is often called a "non-apology apology." It's a way to "accept responsibility" while deflecting blame. It's closely related to the "mistakes were made" rhetorical device, in which errors are acknowledged in the abstract, using the passive voice. Political consultant William Schneider wryly calls this the "past exonerative" tense.[64]

Richard Nixon used the "mistakes were made" gambit during Watergate. Ronald Reagan used it in referring to the Iran-Contra affair.[65] The CEO of JP Morgan Chase acknowledged "mistakes were made" regarding hefty executive bonuses paid from taxpayer-supplied funds.[66]

We should take *personal* responsibility for everything that happens on our watch—even mistakes of subordinates. Great leaders say, "The buck stops here"—and mean it.

> *You say, "I am innocent; he is not angry with me."*
> *But I will pass judgment on you because you say, "I have not sinned."*
> JEREMIAH 2:35

The Power of Quiet Leadership

Don't dismiss the quiet leaders.
Make sure that the quiet leaders are heard and acknowledged.
KARL MOORE

The stereotypical leader is a forceful extrovert who takes charge in every situation. But Adam Grant of the Wharton School cautions us not to ignore the quiet leaders among us.

Grant worked with a university call center that contacted alumni by phone to solicit scholarship donations. Workers read a script, were often hung up on, and collected about one donation per hundred calls made. Morale was low and turnover high.

So Grant brought in scholarship students to speak to the workers and motivate them. The first student was a born leader, full of charisma and enthusiasm. After he spoke, employees made more calls and brought in more donations.

Then Grant brought in a second speaker, an introvert with an excellent academic record but little charisma. The impact was astonishing. Workers almost doubled the number of calls made per day. Donations soared. Grant concluded that extroverts are so focused on being the center of attention that they are not inspiring to others.[67]

Karl Moore of McGill University agrees: "Introverted leaders can add great value to a firm and have important qualities that extroverts lack, so make sure they are heard. Introverted leaders may be more quiet, but...are often more reflective."[68]

Leaders come in many varieties. Don't neglect the power of quiet leadership.

"Take my yoke upon you and learn from me, for I am gentle
and humble in heart, and you will find rest for your souls."
MATTHEW 11:29

Be Bold! Speak Your Mind!

Believest thou? Then thou wilt speak boldly. Speakest thou boldly?
Then thou must suffer. Sufferest thou? Then thou shalt be comforted.
MARTIN LUTHER

Winston Churchill called US Army General George C. Marshall "the organizer of victory" in World War II. After the war, Marshall, as secretary of state, formulated the Marshall Plan for rebuilding postwar Europe. He received the Nobel Peace Prize in 1953.

In 1938, as Adolf Hitler threatened war in Europe, President Franklin D. Roosevelt convened his top military advisers, including General Marshall, head of the Army's War Plans Division. Roosevelt said he wanted to produce ten thousand warplanes in two years, and ten thousand more per year thereafter.

FDR's military advisors all knew that the president hadn't taken into account the logistical support needed for so many planes. Yet none of Roosevelt's advisors dared voice any opposition to Roosevelt's goal—except one man.

After laying out his goals, Roosevelt turned to Marshall and said, "Don't you think so, George?"

The general replied, "Mr. President, I don't agree with that at all." And he proceeded to explain the flaws in FDR's plan. The other officials thought Marshall had just scuttled his career. But one year later, on the very day Hitler invaded Poland, President Roosevelt made George Marshall his Army Chief of Staff, a post Marshall held for the duration of the war.[69]

Great leaders speak their minds. They are focused on leading, not on protecting their careers. Leaders can't be yes-men. Leaders must be bold.

> *"Now, Lord, consider their threats and enable your*
> *servants to speak your word with great boldness."*
> ACTS 4:29

Great Leaders Are "Bag Boys"

He who is not a good servant will not be a good master.
PLATO

Jim Donald is CEO of Extended Stay America. Employed fulltime since age sixteen, he started as a bag boy in a Publix supermarket. By age nineteen, he was an Albertsons assistant manager and owned a home.

Wal-Mart founder Sam Walton learned of Donald's reputation and flew to Phoenix to persuade him to head up Wal-Mart's grocery division. Donald went on to executive positions at Safeway, Pathmark, and Starbucks.

When an interviewer asked Donald the biggest lesson he had learned, he replied, "I worked for [Publix founder] George Jenkins, [Albertsons founder] Joe Albertson, and Sam Walton in my career and they all taught me the same thing: The customer is what matters. . . . How you treat them determines the success of your business."

Donald never lost the servant attitude of a bag boy. "I was being interviewed by *Forbes* recently," he said, "when somebody spilled a drink. I quickly found a mop and cleaned it up. The reporter asked how I knew where to find a mop. I told her: 'A supermarket guy always knows where the closest mop is.'"

Great leaders are "bag boys" at heart. How about you? If you saw a spill, could you find the mop?

"For who is greater, the one who is at the table or the one who serves? Is it not the one who is at the table? But I am among you as one who serves."
LUKE 22:27

The Visionary Leader Advantage

Vision is the art of seeing what is invisible to others.
JONATHAN SWIFT

In *Becoming a Coaching Leader*, Daniel Harkavy, CEO of Building Champions, Inc., describes what he calls "the visionary leader advantage."

"Visionary leaders are better able to make good decisions than those who lack a clear vision.... The clarity of their vision gives them increased confidence; they seldom get confused about what to do next....

"Visionary leaders communicate their vision with excellence. They clearly convey their purpose, convictions, and direction.... Their conviction and confidence causes others to want to be part of their vision....

"Visionary leaders are full of passion, excited about the opportunity ahead. They are passionate about what they're building or bringing to market, passionate about working with the team they've selected, and passionate about making a contribution to their community or society....

"Because they can see what they're going to build five, ten, or even twenty years down the road, they know what they must do to leverage the strengths and talents of their teammates.... Visionary leaders devote a good percentage of their time to leadership development."[70]

What is the visionary advantage you need to harness? Greater confidence? Greater clarity? More effective communication? More passion? Greater commitment to developing new leaders? Ask God for a vision that will energize and empower you as a leader.

Where there is no prophetic vision the people cast off restraint,
but blessed is he who keeps the law.
PROVERBS 29:18 ESV

Your Position Magnifies Every Word You Say

Everything a leader does is symbolic. Everything is amplified.
"If the chairman asks for a cup of coffee," runs an old joke at General Electric,
"someone is liable to go out and buy Brazil."
THOMAS A. STEWART

Dr. Deborah Dunsire is CEO of Millennium, a pharmaceutical company. She learned the power of the CEO title from an executive who offered this metaphor: "You have this megaphone attached to your shoulder that amplifies everything you do."

She found it to be true. She used to wear a worried-looking frown when thinking deeply. People would greet her and she would reply distractedly, still frowning. Then she learned that people were reading more into her distracted expression than she realized. Some people would become alarmed, fearing her frown meant bad news.

"I learned to engage more when people ask me how I am," she says. "People will ask me how I am, and I'll say, 'I'm great and here's why.' ... You don't want your talent thinking that either you're not interested in them, you're angry with them, or the business is going badly.... I've learned to overcommunicate in a way I never did before."[71]

Your people take their cues from you—and your leadership position amplifies everything you do and say. As you communicate, be aware of your magnified impact on the people around you.

Let your conversation be always full of grace, seasoned with salt,
so that you may know how to answer everyone.
COLOSSIANS 4:6

Raising the Roof

I believe in the forgiveness of sin and the redemption of ignorance.
ADLAI E. STEVENSON

In 1963, when twenty-eight-year-old Jack Welch was in his third year at General Electric, he blew up a factory—an inauspicious start for the future CEO of GE.

Welch was in charge of a chemical experiment that went wrong, producing an explosion that blew the roof off the factory. He was in his office, a hundred yards from the factory, when he heard the blast. "It was," he recalls, "one of the most frightening experiences of my life."

The next day, Welch drove to Connecticut to face his boss's boss, Charlie Reed. "I was a nervous wreck," Welch recalls. "I didn't know Charlie Reed that well. Yet from the first minute I walked into his office in Bridgeport, Reed made me feel completely at ease. . . . He took an almost Socratic approach in dealing with the accident. His concern was what I had learned from the explosion."

Reed told Welch, "It's better that we learned about this problem now, rather than later when we had a large-scale operation going. Thank God no one was hurt."

Jack Welch later reflected: "When people make mistakes, the last thing they need is discipline. It's time for encouragement and confidence building. The job at this point is to restore self-confidence."[72]

That's true leadership wisdom—a lesson learned by blowing the roof off a factory.

Brothers and sisters, if someone is caught in a sin,
you who live by the Spirit should restore that person gently.
GALATIANS 6:1

Barnabas, a Leader of Character

*Our chief want is someone who will inspire us t
o be what we know we could be.*
RALPH WALDO EMERSON

In the book of Acts, we meet a leader named Barnabas. Originally called Joseph, his positive, caring personality earned him the nickname *Bar Nabas*, "Son of Encouragement." Acts describes Barnabas as "a good man, full of the Holy Spirit and faith" (Acts 11:24). He was also a generous man, who sold his real estate holdings and donated the proceeds to the church (Acts 4:36–37).

We see the courage of Barnabas in Acts 9. There, Saul, the persecutor of the church, encounters Jesus Christ on the road to Damascus. When Saul comes to Jerusalem, the Christians fear him. They think Saul's conversion is a trick. Barnabas alone dares to meet with Saul and introduce him to the apostles.

In Acts 15, as Paul and Barnabas prepare for their second missionary journey, Barnabas wants to take his cousin Mark with them; Paul refuses. Mark abandoned them on their first journey, so Paul doesn't trust him. Barnabas the encourager clashes with Paul the pragmatist—and the two go their separate ways.

Years later, Paul changes his mind and writes to Timothy from prison, "Get Mark and bring him with you, because he is helpful to me in my ministry" (2 Timothy 4:11).

As leaders, let's be encouragers, willing to take risks to show people we believe in them. When people let us down, let's give them another chance. Odds are they'll vindicate our trust.

Encourage one another daily.
HEBREWS 3:13

The Team Is the Leader

Authentic leaders disciple others who become leaders who disciple others.
Michael Youssef

Retired NBA coach Phil Jackson once said, "The team itself must be the leader of the team."[73] But how can the team lead itself? Longtime NFL coach Marty Schottenheimer explains: "The most successful teams that I've been around were those where the players drove the machine. I'm not talking about during the game. I'm talking about in the locker room, in the meeting room, and on the practice field. Certain conditions were set. And they weren't set by the coaches as much as they were by the players themselves. There was a level of expectation in terms of preparation, effort, and so forth. If certain players fell short, the other guys were quick to say, 'Get with it.'

"That direction is much more effective coming from another player than coming from a coach. . . . A coach can scream and holler about teamwork, but the teams that really have it are the ones on which the players live it and demand it every day. It comes with mutual respect and internal leadership."[74]

Great leaders don't just attract followers. They inspire followers to become leaders. They empower followers to motivate and coach each other, and even to correct each other. Do your job right, and your team itself will become the leader of the team.

So at the Lord's command Moses sent them out from the Desert of Paran.
All of them were leaders of the Israelites.
Numbers 13:3

Washington the Encourager

*Courage is contagious. When a brave man takes a stand,
the spines of others are often stiffened.*
Billy Graham

On December 12, 1799, George Washington braved a blizzard, inspecting his plantation on horseback. The next morning, he awoke with a painful throat and severe hoarseness. Later, he struggled to breathe.

On the morning of December 14, Martha Washington sent for Dr. James Craig, who came and diagnosed the former president with "inflammatory quinsy." Two more doctors arrived and they proceeded to "bleed" Washington several times. They drew about half a pint each time. Once, when the doctor hesitated to make the incision, Washington said, "Don't be afraid."

The doctors tried numerous treatments that weakened Washington and increased his suffering. He told them, "I pray you to take no more trouble about me, let me go off quietly; I cannot last long." The doctors, however, could not accept his death, and continued to torment him with their knives and potions.

The last "bleeding" the doctors administered produced a sluggish flow of blood. Washington's body was shutting down.

Finally, Washington spoke his last words, "'Tis well." He put one hand to his wrist to check his own pulse—then his arms fell slack. He died as he had lived, encouraging and emboldening others. It's a great way to live, and a fine way to die.

*God is our refuge and strength, an ever-present help in trouble.
Therefore we will not fear, though the earth give way
and the mountains fall into the heart of the sea.*

Psalm 46:1–2

A Defiant Helping Hand

A leader should aim to build a life based on service,
not a career based on advancing up the series of positions.
James M. Strock

The International Olympic Committee awarded the 1936 Summer Olympics to Berlin two years before the Nazis came to power. Hitler saw the Olympics as a way to promote Nazism and tried (unsuccessfully) to bar Jews and blacks from participating.

The star of the Berlin games was an African-American, Jesse Owens, who won four gold medals. Owens's chief rival was German long jumper Carl "Luz" Long, who held the European long jump record. Long was eager to compete against Owens, the American record holder.

Owens fouled in his first two attempts by stepping past the takeoff board. He had one more shot at the finals—and his confidence was shaken. So Luz Long offered Owens a suggestion: Jump from a spot *behind* the takeoff board. Owens took Long's advice, made the jump, and advanced to the finals.

Jesse Owens went on to win gold with a jump of 8.06 meters. Luz won the silver. After Owens's winning jump, Long embraced him and put an arm around him as they walked to the locker room—under Hitler's angry glare.

Luz Long became a corporal in the German Army in WWII, and was killed in Sicily in 1943. But on a summer day in 1936, he took a servant-leader's stand against hatred and gave a helping hand to a friend.

"Greater love has no one than this: to lay down one's life for one's friends."
John 15:13

"The Vision Thing"

*Throughout the centuries, there were men who took first steps,
down new roads, armed with nothing but their own vision.*

AYN RAND

Ronald Reagan had a vision for his presidency: (1) fix the economy, (2) restore the military, and (3) end the Cold War. His vice president and successor, George H. W. Bush, never seemed to grasp the importance of vision.

Time reporter Robert Ajemian reported in 1987 that a Bush friend suggested the vice president "go alone to Camp David for a few days to figure out where he wanted to take the country. 'Oh,' said Bush in clear exasperation, 'the vision thing.'"[75]

In 2000, a professor asked Mr. Bush his views on visionary leadership. He replied, "Part of being seen as a visionary is being able to have flowing rhetoric, and… coming out of the clouds and being quoted all the time. My vision was for a kinder and gentler nation, my vision was for more freedom, more democracy around the world.… [I] wasn't particularly good at…rhetoric that can rally people along the way. And so maybe that's part of why I was hit on the vision thing."[76]

Vision is not about rhetorical flourishes. Vision means having a clear, compelling dream of a better future—and communicating that dream with passion and enthusiasm. To be a leader, master "the vision thing."

*"Now I have come to explain to you what will happen to your people
in the future, for the vision concerns a time yet to come."*

DANIEL 10:14

Don't Be a Bore

Boring people don't have to stay that way.
Hedy Lamarr

Tiger Management founder Julian Robertson was a bore and didn't know it. One night, after a cocktail party, his sister told him, "You're becoming a business bore. No one is interested in talking all night long about stocks."

So he made up his mind to stop being a bore. He found other subjects to talk about and stopped pushing his business opinions. He was astonished to find that people became *more* interested in his market advice. "I was a broker starting out," he says, "and it helped me acquire clients."[77]

Because leaders wield authority, few people dare to say, "You know, your speech tonight bored everyone to tears." Fortunately for Julian Robertson, his sister cared enough to speak the truth.

There are many ways that leaders bore others without realizing it. Julian Robertson bored people by being a man of one subject. When he expanded his horizons, he became a sparkling conversationalist.

Leaders sometimes bore by going on too long. Voltaire said, "The best way to be boring is to leave nothing out." Leaders also bore by talking only of themselves. Ask questions and get people to talk about themselves—they'll think you're fascinating!

To be a great leader, obey the first law of communication: Never be a bore.

"People listened to me expectantly, waiting in silence for my counsel.
After I had spoken, they spoke no more; my words fell gently on their ears.
They waited for me as for showers and drank in my words as the spring rain."
Job 29:21–23

The Leader Who Empathizes

Empathy is not only the ability to listen and understand other people.
It's also the skill of crawling into another person's way of thinking.
RON WILLINGHAM

Psychologist Carl Rogers, who pioneered client-centered therapy, writes, "The most powerful persuasive force in interpersonal relations is the ability…to perceive how another person feels."[78] The "persuasive force" he speaks of is called *empathy*.

An empathetic leader cares about the thoughts and feelings of others. Empathy is not sympathy—feeling sorry for others. Empathy is an understanding of the needs and motives of others. It's the ability to appreciate another person's experience, perception, and reasons for doing what they do.

It takes effort to empathize. Many busy leaders won't take the time to understand how their followers think and feel. Empathy is by definition unselfish, so you have to put others ahead of yourself in order to show empathy.

While empathy sounds selfless and altruistic, it is actually beneficial to the leader and the organization. Followers who feel the leader understands, supports, and listens to them are more highly motivated than those who feel ignored and misunderstood.

Empathy builds trust, strengthens relationships, and improves cooperation. An empathetic leader can turn struggling followers into overachievers. Just as Jesus empathized with our hurts and weaknesses, our leadership should be characterized by empathy for others.

For we do not have a high priest who is unable to empathize
with our weaknesses, but we have one who has been tempted
in every way, just as we are—yet he did not sin.

HEBREWS 4:15

An Award for Integrity

Character is much easier kept than recovered.
THOMAS PAINE

Bobby Jones was an amateur golfer (an attorney by profession) best known for founding Augusta National Golf Club and the Masters Tournament, and for winning all four of golf's major tournaments—the Grand Slam—in 1930. He's also famous for his integrity.

At the eleventh hole of the first round of the 1925 US Open, Jones prepared to pitch out of the rough and onto the green. When his club flicked the grass, the ball moved slightly. No one saw but Jones. He took the shot and told the official to add a penalty stroke. The official argued against the penalty, but Jones insisted. The penalty cost Jones an outright win in regulation, and he lost in the playoff.

After sportswriters praised Jones for his sportsmanlike integrity, he replied, "You might as well praise a man for not robbing a bank."

The next year, in the second round of the 1926 Open, Jones was on the fifteenth green. The course was windy, and as he grounded his putter to square up for the putt, a wind gust jostled the ball. No one saw but Jones. Again, he called a penalty on himself. This time, however, Jones went on to win.

The United States Golf Association created a sportsmanship award in 1955 and called it the Bob Jones Award. If your peers named an award for you, would it be a testament to your character?

The LORD detests lying lips, but he delights in people who are trustworthy.
PROVERBS 12:22

Leaders Build More Leaders

Leaders don't create followers; they create more leaders.
TOM PETERS

Jesus didn't call His twelve disciples to be *followers*. He called them, trained them, and sent them out as *leaders*. Jesus selected the twelve (with the exception of Judas) as the nucleus of His new church.

Did Jesus see leadership potential in each one? Or did He choose twelve ordinary men at random? I believe Jesus carefully sized up each man's traits and abilities before He said, "Follow me."

When Jesus called Andrew, He knew Andrew was already following John the Baptist (John 1:35–40), so this man was an earnest seeker of truth. Andrew's brother, Simon Peter, stood out as a bold, take-charge individual, the self-appointed spokesmen for the twelve. Like many "born leaders," Peter had many rough edges.

Matthew the tax collector was an odd choice. The Jews despised tax collectors for serving the hated Roman government. Yet Jesus transformed Matthew's chief flaw (ambition for money) into a virtue (ambition for God).

Jesus saw leadership potential in the stormy personalities of James and John, whom He called "the sons of thunder." And Jesus viewed the radical intensity of Simon the Zealot as a leadership qualification. Jesus undoubtedly saw many unique leadership traits in each of the twelve disciples.

That's our challenge as leaders—to recognize ability, to train and inspire people, and to send them out as leaders in their own right. Great leaders like Jesus don't just attract followers; they build more leaders.

"Come, follow me," Jesus said, "and I will send you out to fish for people."
MATTHEW 4:19

Steady under Fire

The key to winning is poise under stress.
PAUL BROWN

Admiral Raymond Spruance commanded the American carrier forces in the Battle of Midway during World War II. His colleagues nicknamed him "Electric Brain" for being calm in a crisis.

Before Midway, Admiral Spruance had never commanded aircraft carriers and hundreds of planes in battle. But when carrier force commander Admiral William Halsey fell sick, he recommended Spruance, then an escort commander, as his replacement.

Spruance commanded a three-carrier group against a much stronger Japanese force with four carriers. Japan planned to capture the Midway Islands, then invade Hawaii and push the American fleet out of the Pacific.

On June 4, 1942, Japanese bombers attacked Midway—and Spruance launched a daring gambit. Despite the extreme range, Spruance ordered planes to pursue the enemy back to their carriers. The American dive-bombers caught the enemy in the midst of rearming to attack the US carriers. Lacking air cover, all four Japanese carriers were sunk or crippled. Had the American attack failed, the US carriers would have been wide open to a counterattack.

As journalist Scott S. Smith concludes, "Spruance's Midway lesson is that staying calm while taking calculated risks can trump disadvantages."[79] In your leadership crises, learn from the "Electric Brain." Be strategically bold, yet steady under fire.

With bitterness archers attacked him; they shot at him with hostility. But his bow remained steady, his strong arms stayed limber, because of the hand of the Mighty One of Jacob, because of the Shepherd, the Rock of Israel.
GENESIS 49:23–24

"We Must Serve or We Die"

People who give will never be poor!
Anne Frank

The late Dr. Paul Brand spent his career serving leprosy patients in India. He told writer Philip Yancey the story of Pierre, a former member of the French Parliament. During one harsh winter, Pierre worried that the Parisian beggars would freeze to death. So he joined a religious order and began organizing the beggars.

Pierre taught the beggars to build a warehouse from discarded bricks. Then he divided them into teams. They fanned out into the city, picking up used bottles from hotels and restaurants to recycle them. Pierre made each beggar responsible to help someone poorer than himself.

The effort was so successful that soon there were few beggars left in the city—they had all become productive recyclers. Pierre worried about the future of the beggars when they ran out of people to serve.

So he went to India, where he found many beggars infected with leprosy, members of the "untouchable" caste. Returning to France, he mobilized the French beggars and took them to India, where they built a leprosy ward for the hospital in Vellore. When the leprosy patients wanted to thank Pierre and his team for building the ward, Pierre replied, "It is you who have saved us. We must serve or we die."[80]

> *"In everything I did, I showed you that by this kind of hard work we must help the weak, remembering the words the Lord Jesus himself said: 'It is more blessed to give than to receive.'"*
>
> Acts 20:35

Why Do You Want to Lead?

*Great achievement is usually born of great sacrifice, a
nd is never the result of selfishness.*
Napoleon Hill

Patrick Lencioni is founder and president of The Table Group. He is in great
demand as an author, speaker, and consultant on leadership and organiza-
tional dynamics. He once observed: "When I hear a young person say glibly that
he or she wants to be a leader someday, I feel compelled to ask the question 'why?'

"If the answer is 'because I want to make a difference' or 'I want to change the
world,' I get a little skeptical and have to ask a follow-up question: 'Why and in
what way do you want to change the world?' If they struggle to answer that question, I discourage them from becoming a leader.

"Why? Because a leader who doesn't know why he or she wants to lead is
almost always motivated by self-interest."

Lencioni goes on to explain that authentic leadership requires selflessness
and vision. Those who want to lead but have no vision are simply ambitious for
power, fame, or wealth. Such people have no interest in sacrificing themselves for
the greater good. They are simply on an ego trip.

Leaders are visionaries and must be willing to sacrifice for their vision. Few
understand the sacrificial and visionary nature of leadership—"which explains,"
says Lencioni, "why leadership is a rare trait in society, and always has been."

*"For even the Son of Man did not come to be served,
but to serve, and to give his life as a ransom for many."*
Mark 10:45

One of the Most Rewarding Leadership Tasks

Teaching is at the heart of leading. . . .
If you aren't teaching, you aren't leading.
NOEL M. TICHY AND ELI B. COHEN
THE LEADERSHIP ENGINE

Before serving as secretary of state, Condoleezza Rice taught political science at Stanford University. One of her students recalls that many students "wanted to be like her. This was not idle hero worship. She seemed to be the embodiment of everything we admired about academia. She was knowledgeable without being closed-minded, prestigious without being pompous, and her lectures were complex without being dry."[81]

Professor Rice began her teaching career in 1981 as a twenty-six-year-old assistant professor at Stanford. A fellow professor recalls being impressed by her "charm and very gracious personality. . .a kind of intellectual agility mixed with velvet-glove forcefulness. She's a steel magnolia."[82] Another colleague calls her "a very effective leader, decisive, clear-headed."[83]

Condi Rice taught leadership principles through role-playing. She'd have her class reenact foreign-policy crises, with students acting as presidents, premiers, and diplomats. As students made decisions and negotiated, they learned how complex and difficult foreign-policy problems can be. After playing the role of a Soviet defense minister, a student said it was "the most intense week I've ever had."[84]

One of the most rewarding tasks of leadership is teaching the *next* generation of leaders. Great leaders teach; great teachers lead.

When Jesus landed and saw a large crowd, he had compassion on them, because they were like sheep without a shepherd. So he began teaching them many things.
MARK 6:34

Tend to Their Psyches

Your career success in the workplace of today—independent of technical expertise—depends on the quality of your people skills.
MAX MESSMER

Psychologist Daniel Goleman is the author of the 1995 bestseller *Emotional Intelligence*. Goleman discusses the people skills of former Yankees manager Joe Torre.

"During the 1999 World Series, Torre tended ably to the psyches of his players as they endured the emotional pressure cooker of a pennant race. All season long, he made a special point to praise Scott Brosius, whose father had died during the season, for staying committed even as he mourned. . . . After the team's final game, Torre specifically sought out right fielder Paul O'Neill. . .[who played after receiving] news of his father's death that morning. . . . Torre made a point of acknowledging O'Neill's personal struggle, calling him a 'warrior.'

"Torre also used the spotlight of the victory celebration to praise two players whose return the following year was threatened by contract disputes. In doing so, he sent a clear message to the team and to the club's owner that he valued the players immensely—too much to lose them."[85]

Whether you lead a team, a company, a military unit, or a church, you'll be more effective if you tend to the psyches of your followers. Get to know them. Listen to them. Affirm them. Mourn with them and celebrate with them.

Then watch them become champions.

Therefore encourage one another and build each other up,
just as in fact you are doing.
1 THESSALONIANS 5:11

Moses: The Character Traits of a Deliverer

*Moses was the greatest legislator and the commander in chief
of perhaps the first liberation army.*
ELIE WIESEL

Hebrews 11 lists the key leadership traits of Moses the Deliverer:
"By faith Moses...refused to be known as the son of Pharaoh's daughter" (verse 24). Moses refused to be identified with the world's false values.

"He chose to be mistreated along with the people of God rather than to enjoy the fleeting pleasures of sin" (verse 25). Moses chose to align himself with God's plan. Though raised an Egyptian, Moses boldly identified himself with God's people.

"He regarded disgrace for the sake of Christ as of greater value than the treasures of Egypt, because he was looking ahead to his reward" (verse 26). Moses was a leader of vision; he was focused on a future reward. Deuteronomy 34:7 says that Moses died at age 120, yet "his eyes were not weak." His strong physical vision symbolized his unfailing spiritual vision.

"By faith...he persevered because he saw him who is invisible" (verse 27). Moses was persistent. There was no quit in him, because his eyes were fixed on God.

Moses is a role model of leadership for you and me. Let's follow his example and lead by rejecting the false values of this world, by aligning ourselves with God's purpose, by maintaining our spiritual vision, and by persistently keeping our eyes fixed on God.

*[Jesus said], "If you believed Moses, you would believe me,
for he wrote about me."*
JOHN 5:46

Opposites Need Each Other

*Many successful ventures are the result of effective
partnerships between introverts and extroverts.*
SUSAN CAIN

High school buddies Ben Cohen and Jerry Greenfield opened their first ice cream shop in 1978. Jerry, the introvert, ran the shop and manufactured the ice cream. Ben, the extrovert, marketed the Ben and Jerry's brand. Together, they made an unbeatable team.

We see the same dynamic in the founders of Apple Computers. Outgoing and charismatic Steve Jobs perfectly complemented his brilliant-yet-introverted partner, Steve Wozniak. The pairing of these two opposites produced one of the greatest companies of all time.

The pattern is repeated in Microsoft cofounders Bill Gates (extroverted marketing genius and deal maker) and Paul Allen (introverted manager and tech innovator). We see this pattern in Hewlett-Packard cofounders David Packard (driven extrovert) and William Hewlett (easygoing introvert). We see it again in the relationship between Walt Disney (imaginative extroverted genius) and his brother Roy (pragmatic introverted financier). As Disney expert Peggy Matthews Rose told me, "Every Walt needs a Roy and every Roy needs a Walt."

Orlando Magic co-owner Rich DeVos cofounded Amway with Jay Van Andel. Rich was the extroverted salesman, while Jay was the introverted problem-solver. Rich and Jay magnified each other's strengths and compensated for each other's weaknesses.

In your leadership life, merge your strengths with someone who complements you, then go out and conquer the world together.

*There are many parts, but one body. The eye cannot say to the hand, "I don't
need you!" And the head cannot say to the feet, "I don't need you!"*
1 CORINTHIANS 12:20–21

Sitting Down to Take a Stand

Even God lends a hand to honest boldness.
MENANDER

Isabella Baumfree was a great evangelist and abolitionist who was born into slavery. While a slave, she suffered many beatings and indignities. In 1826, she escaped from an Ulster County, New York, estate with her infant daughter. (New York outlawed slavery the following year.) Later, she successfully sued her former master and recovered her son.

During the Civil War, Baumfree, who was now known as Sojourner Truth, recruited black soldiers for the Union Army. In 1864, President Abraham Lincoln invited her to the White House and thanked her. That same year, Congress passed a resolution abolishing segregated streetcars in Washington, DC—a resolution that trolley conductors routinely disobeyed.

One day in 1865, Sojourner Truth stood on a Washington street corner and signaled to a horse-drawn trolley to stop. When the conductor ignored her, she shouted, "I want to ride! I want to ride!" When a crowd assembled, blocking the street and forcing the conductor to halt, Sojourner Truth leaped aboard.

The surly conductor told her to ride up front by the horses—but instead she sat down among the white passengers. "As a citizen of the Empire State of New York," she said, "I know the law as well as you do."

After riding the trolley to the end of the line, she exclaimed, "Bless God! I have had a ride!"

Some great leaders sit down to take a bold stand for the truth.

The wicked flee though no one pursues,
but the righteous are as bold as a lion.
PROVERBS 28:1

Be a Leader—Be a Servant

*A leader is one who, out of madness or goodness, volunteers
to take upon himself the woe of the people.*
JOHN UPDIKE

The seventh side of leadership—A Serving Heart—is actually woven throughout the other six sides.

We serve our followers through *Vision*—a dream of a future that benefits everyone. We serve our followers through *Communication* as we share hope and inspiration. We demonstrate love and caring through *People Skills*. We set an example through good *Character*. We inspire confidence through our *Competence*. We courageously blaze a trail through our *Boldness*. Ultimately, everything we do as leaders comes from the seventh side of leadership: *A Serving Heart*.

Jesus told His followers: "Whoever wants to become great among you must be your servant, and whoever wants to be first must be slave of all. For even the Son of Man did not come to be served, but to serve, and to give his life as a ransom for many" (Mark 10:43–45).

Hours before the cross, while Jesus and the twelve disciples were sharing the Passover meal, an argument broke out. Each of the disciples wanted to be the boss. So Jesus filled a basin with water, took up a towel, and went from man to man, washing each disciple's feet. His example of servanthood silenced all argument.

Remember the example of Jesus: If you want to lead, you've got to serve. If you don't understand serving, you don't understand leadership. So be a leader—be a servant.

Serve wholeheartedly, as if you were serving the Lord, not people.
EPHESIANS 6:7

Making Boyhood Dreams Come True

*Lillian used to say, "But why do you want to build an amusement park?
They're so dirty." I told her that was just the point—mine wouldn't be.*
WALT DISNEY

In Walt Disney's *Pinocchio*, Jiminy Cricket sings, "If your heart is in your dream, no request is too extreme." Walt Disney put his heart into his dreams, especially the dream called Disneyland.

Walt's dream began during his boyhood in Kansas City, at Electric Park—a huge amusement park with thrill rides and fireworks, named for the one hundred thousand electric bulbs that nightly transformed it into a fantasyland. Too poor to afford the ten-cent admission, Walt often peered through the fence, imagining the wonders inside.

Twenty years later, in 1932, Walt began drawing plans for Disneyland. His vision gained momentum when he took his daughters to Griffith Park in Los Angeles. As his daughters rode the merry-go-round, Walt sat on a bench and wished there were a place where families could have fun *together*.

He visited amusement parks around the world and hired experts to do feasibility studies. His brother and business partner, Roy Disney, tried to dissuade him—to no avail. Walt sold his vacation home, borrowed against his life insurance, and sent Roy to find investors—and then he began building his boyhood vision.

When you visit a Disney park, remember you are living inside the dreams of that boy who stood outside the fence at Electric Park. What dreams of your youth do you want to build?

"Your beginnings will seem humble, so prosperous will your future be."
JOB 8:7

Leaders Are Storytellers

The shortest distance between two people is a story.
TERRENCE GARGIULO

Steve Sabol helped found NFL Films with his father, Ed Sabol. He began working as a writer, editor, and cameraman with the 1962 NFL Championship game. Over the years, Steve won more than forty Emmy Awards as a documentary filmmaker, and succeeded his father as president of the company.

More than a filmmaker, Steve Sabol was a storyteller. He used camera angles, slow-motion images, stirring music, the shouts of players, and the collision of helmets to transform football games into epic tales of human drama.

In March 2011, Sabol learned he had inoperable brain cancer. In August of that year, he delivered an emotional introduction at the Hall of Fame enshrinement of his ninety-four-year-old father. And on September 18, 2012, Steve passed away at age sixty-nine.

When his father's Hall of Fame induction was announced, Steve said, "My dad has a great expression: 'Tell me a fact, and I'll learn. Tell me a truth, and I'll believe. But tell me a story, and it will live in my heart forever.'"[86]

That is great leadership wisdom. Our greatest leaders have always been storytellers. They use stories to illustrate their vision, teach us lessons, touch our emotions, rivet our attention, and motivate us to action. Stories move us, compel us, and inspire us. Stories make us laugh—and cry.

To be persuasive, to be unforgettable, simply say, "Let me tell you a story...."

Starting from the beginning, Peter told them the whole story.
ACTS 11:4

"An Incredibly Gracious Act"

There are two types of people—those who come into a room and say, "Well, here I am!" and those who come in and say, "Ah, there you are."
FREDERICK L. COLLINS

In *The Natural*, Joe Klein writes that President Bill Clinton's "public charm. . . will doubtless stand as his most memorable quality." Klein defines that quality as "his ability to talk, to empathize, to understand; his willingness to fall behind schedule, to infuriate his staff, merely because some stray citizen on a rope line had a problem or a story that needed to be heard."

Klein relates a story told by Senator Paul Wellstone, whose friend Dennis Wadley had terminal cancer in 1994. Wellstone arranged for President Clinton to meet Wadley.

"Clinton came right over to us," Wellstone recalled, "and he immediately sized up the situation—Dennis didn't want to talk about his disease, he wanted to have a policy discussion. And the president stood there, for forty-five minutes, and gave Dennis the gift of taking him seriously, listening to him. . . . It was an incredibly gracious act."

Klein lamented "the larger sense of incompleteness that haunted" the Clinton presidency due to the Lewinsky scandal and the "gush of pardons granted on his last night in office."[87] All true. But in people skills, Bill Clinton had few equals.

A leader with strong people skills plus strong character would be an amazingly influential leader—and an example worth emulating.

Finally, all of you, be like-minded, be sympathetic, love one another, be compassionate and humble.
1 PETER 3:8

Joshua: The Faithful Warrior

*Faithfulness in a few things is the condition of rule over many things;
and the loyalty of a servant is the stepping-stone to the royalty of the throne.*
F. B. Meyer

Over the years, military historians have scoured the book of Joshua for the secret to Joshua's battlefield success. They've tried to understand how this former slave could lead Israel to victory over the Canaanite hordes.

The secret is. . .*there is no secret*! The Israelites won *not* by strength of arms or strategic superiority. They won because Joshua was faithful to God.

When Joshua led the Israelites across the Jordan River, he had no Army Corps of Engineers to build a pontoon bridge. He simply had faith. The Lord told Joshua to send the priests with the Ark of the Covenant toward the river. In faith, Joshua obeyed. As the priests reached the river, the waters parted and the people crossed on dry land.

God told Israel to march around Jericho for seven days, and then blow trumpets (Joshua 6). What kind of military strategy is that? Yet Joshua obeyed and the walls fell. Later, God stopped the sun in the sky, giving Israel extra daylight to defeat the Amorites (Joshua 10).

Joshua was not a genius at strategy. He was simply faithful to God. The Lord still seeks faithful leaders who are obedient to His will. Follow God's strategy and He will take care of the victory.

"Be strong and courageous, because you will lead these people."
Joshua 1:6

The Leader as Master Delegator

A good leader isn't a slave to detail; he uses his valuable time to tackle what's truly important. And this leads to greater success for him and his organization.
Brett and Kate McKay

President Calvin Coolidge brought a unique leadership style to the White House. A master delegator, Coolidge selected highly qualified people to serve in his administration, gave them broad authority, told them what he expected of them, and held them strictly accountable for the results. He was involved and engaged—yet he avoided interfering with the decisions of his people.

Coolidge had seen how his predecessor, Warren G. Harding, had failed to oversee the actions of his corrupt secretary of the interior, resulting in the Teapot Dome scandal. Coolidge would not allow any corruption on his watch. By maintaining a balance of broad delegated authority and strict accountability, Coolidge enjoyed a successful tenure and presided over one of the most prosperous periods in American history.

Take some tips from the example of Calvin Coolidge: Remember that you can delegate tasks but not responsibility—the buck still stops with you. Choose creative, self-motivated people and empower them to make decisions. Set clear goals and standards. Check in with your people on a regular basis. Make sure they achieve the goals you set. Then share the rewards, credit, and praise when the mission is accomplished.

> *"Select capable men from all the people—men who fear God, trustworthy men who hate dishonest gain—and appoint them as officials over thousands, hundreds, fifties, and tens."*
> Exodus 18:21

Boldly Confront Conflict

When human beings live together, conflict is inevitable
DAISAKU IKEDA

Conflict and interpersonal problems are a normal part of any team, organization, faculty, military unit, or church. Effective leaders boldly confront problems for the good of everyone. In *Am I Making Myself Clear?* business leader Terry Felber offers eight principles for mastering the art of confrontation:

1. *Nothing is a big deal.* Any issue can be worked out.

2. *Forgive and forget.* Always stay in the present. Don't dredge up the past.

3. *Keep a low tone of voice and speak slowly.* Keep your emotions in check, even if the other person doesn't. A lowered voice has a calming effect.

4. *Depersonalize everything.* No matter what others say, don't take it personally.

5. *There are two sides to every story.* Your opinion may be based on incomplete information. Be open to other points of view.

6. *Ask for forgiveness.* Even if you've done nothing wrong, you can say, "I'm sorry my words upset you. That wasn't my intention."

7. *Never discuss conflict over the phone.* Important nonverbal cues get lost over the phone. Confront problems face-to-face.

8. *Never confront problems when you're tired.* Difficult discussions go better when everyone is at their best.[88]

> *"If your brother or sister sins, go and point out their fault, just between the two of you. If they listen to you, you have won them over."*
> MATTHEW 18:15

Always Serving the Greater Good

Before you are a leader, success is all about growing yourself.
When you become a leader, success is all about growing others.
JACK WELCH

In *Soldier, Statesman, Peacemaker*, Jack Uldrich reveals leadership lessons from the life of General George C. Marshall. One of Marshall's traits, Uldrich says, was his "unique skill in picking the right people." For example, at the beginning of World War II, Marshall promoted Dwight D. Eisenhower from lieutenant colonel to brigadier general, advancing him ahead of 350 more senior officers.

After the D-Day invasion, led by Eisenhower, it was clear that Marshall had chosen well. Less than a week after the invasion, Marshall went to Europe and held a private conversation with his commanding general. When Marshall asked Eisenhower what qualities he looked for in the people he promoted, Eisenhower replied, "Selflessness"—then added that he had learned that principle from Marshall himself.

In 1953, when Eisenhower became president, he sent General Marshall to England to represent the United States at the coronation of Queen Elizabeth II. As Marshall walked down the aisle of Westminster Abbey beside General Omar Bradley, he noticed row after row of dignitaries on either side standing to their feet.

Marshall whispered to Bradley, "Who are they rising for?" Bradley replied, "You." Uldrich concluded, "The leaders of the free world were standing in his honor because they knew he always served the greater good."[89]

"Choose for yourselves this day whom you will serve. . . .
But as for me and my household, we will serve the LORD."
JOSHUA 24:15

Pick a Number

A big thinker always visualizes what can be done in the future.
He isn't stuck with the present.
DAVID J. SCHWARTZ

In *A Renegade's Guide to God*, the late Rev. David Foster said that a simple game of "pick a number" can tell you a lot about how you think. If asked to pick any number at random, what number would you choose? Would it be less than a million? Most people choose small, familiar numbers. It's a rare individual who envisions a *big* number, because people aren't used to thinking big.

Foster offered this example of the power of thinking big: "In 1998, Larry Page and Sergey Brin incorporated Google while still graduate students at Stanford University. According to *Fortune Small Business* magazine, Internet users perform more than 150 million searches a day on the Google search engine. . . .

"It began with their initial vision. The word 'googol' is a mathematical term for the number one followed by one hundred zeros. While most people are likely to pick a number like fourteen or ninety-eight when doing the 'pick-a-number' test, Brin and Page decided to pick a googol."

A Google executive once said of Page and Brin, "It's rare to find people who think on such a grand scale and are able to create a great product at the same time."[90]

How far will your leadership vision take you?

Now to him who is able to do immeasurably more than all we ask or imagine,
according to his power that is at work within us. . .
EPHESIANS 3:20

Leaders Teach and Correct

*A very important part of leadership is lifting people up and
making them realize they can be better than they are.*
J. RICHARD MUNRO

As recorded in Matthew 16 and Mark 8, Jesus got in a boat with His disciples and went across the lake. Reaching the far shore, Jesus told them, "Be on your guard against the yeast of the Pharisees and Sadducees" (Matthew 16:6).

The disciples were baffled by His talk of "yeast." They whispered, "It is because we didn't bring any bread" (Matthew 16:7).

Aware of their conversation, Jesus said, in effect, "Are you really that dense? Don't you remember that I used a few loaves to feed crowds of thousands, and we gathered baskets of leftovers afterward? Do you really think it's a problem for Me that you forgot to bring bread?"

Jesus had used a figure of speech to teach an important point. The "yeast" referred to the self-righteous pride of the religious rulers. The rulers believed that God cared about rituals; Jesus taught that God cared about relationships. The rulers believed that God was focused on outward appearances; Jesus taught that God cared about the inner reality.

The Lord Jesus wanted to lift the disciples' minds from mundane matters of bread to the eternal reality of spiritual truth. As leaders, we must continually teach and correct our followers, using our communication skills to help them focus on what is truly important.

The disciples went and did as Jesus had instructed them.
MATTHEW 21:6

Leading with Clarity

The bad old days of "sink or swim" are gone forever.
Human assets are too precious to squander.
BRIAN TRACY

In *TurboStrategy*, Brian Tracy observes that in companies with highly motivated, top-performing people, you invariably find "absolute clarity with regard to the results expected." He adds, "In turbulent times, with rapid and discontinuous change all around you, you should continually revisit the job description and the results expected of each person."[91]

Leadership consultant John Baldoni agrees with the importance of clear expectations. He offers a simple three-point checklist to test whether your organization sets clear expectations:

"1. *Do people know what is expected of them?* Too often we assume people know their jobs. . . . People need to be told, and reminded, of the importance of their work.

"2. *Do employees know what they can expect from you?* It is important to let employees know that you as their manager are available to them. . . . For new hires, you might be more teacher than boss. For veterans, you will play the coaching role. For the team, you will be the supplier of resources as well as their champion.

"3. *Do employees know what is expected of each other?* . . . Whether a self-managed team makes its own assignments or a manager makes the assignments, what matters most is that employees know who does what."[92]

To lead effectively, set clear expectations—and repeat them frequently.

If the trumpet does not sound a clear call, who will get ready for battle?
1 CORINTHIANS 14:8

Never "Fudge" Your Character

Business can represent human society at its best. . . . When done ethically,
business quite literally changes the world for the better.
Ben Horowitz

In August 2010, Mark Hurd was forced to resign as CEO of Hewlett-Packard. His removal was criticized by Joe Nocera of the *New York Times*, who claimed Hurd was guilty of nothing more than having "fudged some expense reports." Fudged?

Ben Horowitz, a former HP software executive, uses a different word: *falsified*. "The false expense reports," he explains, "are related to a contractor named Jodie Fisher, a former soft-core porn movie actress. . . . She was hired by Hewlett-Packard and paid up to $5,000 per meeting to meet with Fortune 50 CEOs."

What's the big deal? HP was profitable under Hurd's leadership—isn't that all that matters? Mr. Hurd "fudged" some expense reports—so what?

Ben Horowitz replies that if a CEO of a public company falsifies a financial statement, "he must be fired. . . . This is nonnegotiable." He concludes, "Every person who invests in Hewlett-Packard does so on the basis of HP's financial statements. . . . They trust that the statements are true. . . . Hewlett-Packard's board of directors stood tall and protected the company, its shareholders and all of us. . . . I am extremely proud of and grateful for their actions."[93]

Do you stand tall for your integrity? Is your character nonnegotiable—or do you sometimes "fudge" your ethical standards?

May integrity and uprightness protect me.
Psalm 25:21

Don't Put Policy Ahead of Competence

A leader does not hesitate to cut through red tape, or even bend the rules when necessary, to create better possibilities for the future.
SUE HANSEN

Novelist Lawrence Block tells about a best-selling author who agreed to do a book signing at an independent bookstore. The bookseller's advertising brought in 450 prepaid book orders, guaranteeing a successful signing.

But when the bookseller tried to order 450 books, the publisher's sales rep said, "We can only ship you two hundred." Why? "Company policy."

"But the books are sold," the bookseller explained. "I've got prepaid orders. I'll pay in advance and take them as nonreturnable. There's no risk to you." The publishing house refused to budge from its policy.

The bookseller hung up—then had an idea. He drove four blocks to the nearest Target store. The Target manager happily sold the bookseller three hundred copies at a 45 percent discount (and still made a profit). The book-signing was a huge success.[94]

Was the policy at fault? No, it was undoubtedly a good policy—for most circumstances. The problem was *rigid, incompetent enforcement* of the policy. Fortunately, a competent bookseller and a competent Target manager found a solution for the publisher's incompetence.

Moral: Don't put policy ahead of competence. Rules serve a valid function, but competent leaders know when to make an exception.

He has made us competent as ministers of a new covenant—not of the letter but of the Spirit; for the letter kills, but the Spirit gives life.
2 CORINTHIANS 3:6

With God against Man

With Christ's light let us illuminate even the most hideous caverns of the human person: torture, jail, plunder, want, chronic illness. The oppressed must be saved. . .[by] the holy revolution of the Son of Man.
ARCHBISHOP ÓSCAR ROMERO

In *Moses on Management*, Rabbi David Baron tells the story of Aristides de Sousa Mendes. De Sousa was a Portuguese diplomat serving as consul general in Bordeaux, France, at the beginning of World War II. As Hitler's forces marched through Europe, thousands of Jewish refugees streamed into Bordeaux seeking visas to Portugal, a neutral state.

When Portugal issued a new policy, forbidding visas for Jewish refugees, the devoutly Catholic de Sousa faced a crisis of conscience. Wanting to save the Jewish refugees, he implored his government to revoke the new policy. Receiving no reply, de Sousa took a bold action. He assembled his staff and for three days they stamped visas around the clock.

When Portuguese officials realized what de Sousa had done, they dismissed him and took away his salary and pension. As a result, he died penniless in a charity hospital in 1954—yet Aristides de Sousa Mendes died a hero, having saved thirty thousand Jews. He once said, "I would rather be with God against man than with man against God."[95]

What bold act of conscience and sacrifice is God urging you to take right now?

So we say with confidence, "The Lord is my helper;
I will not be afraid; what can mere mortals do to me?"
HEBREWS 13:6

Leaders Who Serve "the Least of These"

You can only govern men by serving them. The rule is without exception.
Victor Kiam

Prison Fellowship founder Charles Colson told about two special volunteers who served inner-city children at Christmastime in 2003. President George W. Bush and his wife, Laura, went to Shiloh Baptist Church in Alexandria, Virginia, and gave gifts to kids who had one or both parents in prison. Reporters came, shot video, took photos, and left.

"I remember from my days with President Nixon," Colson said, "what photo opportunities are: Get the picture and leave. So I thought the Bushes would shortly depart, but they didn't. They stayed long after the cameras were gone. . . . Though the press didn't report it, I noticed that both the president and Mrs. Bush talked to the Hispanic children in Spanish."

That story never appeared in any newspaper or on any broadcast. Why did the media bury the story? "The president," Colson explained, "is a Christian who really cares for 'the least of these.' . . . That is something that his detractors in the media simply can't handle. . . . It dashes the stereotypes."

The scene, Colson notes, is symbolic: "The most powerful man in the world... had a wonderful visit with the most powerless people in our society." That scene echoes the Christmas story, in which God's Son "came to be with the least powerful."[96] Our servant-leadership should echo that of the King who came as a Servant.

Serve one another humbly in love.
Galatians 5:13

A Vision for the Next Game

Never look directly at the sun. Instead, look at the sunflower.
VERA NAZARIAN

After a successful stint as the Minnesota Vikings' offensive coordinator, Brian Billick became head coach of the Baltimore Ravens. In his first year, Billick coached the Ravens to the first non-losing season (8–8) in the team's four-year history.

In Billick's second season, the Ravens improved to 12–4. During that season, Billick chose not to set a vision for the entire season. Instead, he set a new vision for each game, week by week. He refused to allow players to think further ahead than the next game. He fined any player caught using the words *playoffs* or *Super Bowl.*

In response, the players developed code words, borrowed from TV's *Seinfeld.* They referred to the playoffs as "Festivus" and the Super Bowl as "Festivus Maximus." Billick lifted the word ban once the Ravens advanced to Super Bowl XXXV against the New York Giants. In a lopsided 34–7 contest, Brian Billick and the Baltimore Ravens won their first Super Bowl rings.

In *Competitive Leadership,* Billick writes: "Effective leaders plan for an organization's future by establishing a vision. . . . The vision is the benchmark that keeps everyone on track. It is the touchstone that helps guide the behavior of the leader."[97]

Sometimes the most important vision is the one that takes you through the next game.

> *Know also that wisdom is like honey for you:*
> *If you find it, there is a future hope for you,*
> *and your hope will not be cut off.*
> PROVERBS 24:14

The Weight of a Leader's Words

The Teacher searched to find just the right words,
and what he wrote was upright and true.
ECCLESIASTES 12:10

In *Presidential Courage*, Michael Beschloss tells the story of the June 1963 showdown between President John F. Kennedy and Alabama governor George Wallace. After the courts ordered the University of Alabama to admit black students, Wallace defiantly blocked the doors. JFK responded by federalizing the Alabama National Guard and sending a brigadier general to order Wallace to step aside. The governor complied—and the students entered.

Seeing a teachable moment for the nation, JFK called network officials and asked for broadcast time. Then he assigned speechwriter Ted Sorensen to write a speech. Five minutes before airtime, Sorensen handed Kennedy an unfinished script. Kennedy would have to "wing it" at the end.

JFK went before the TV cameras and said, "One hundred years of delay have passed since President Lincoln freed the slaves, yet their heirs, their grandsons are not fully free. . . . A great change is at hand, and our task—our obligation—is to make that revolution—that change—peaceful and constructive for all."[98] Those words galvanized the nation and built momentum for the Civil Rights Act of 1964.

Great leaders don't keep silent at crucial moments in history. They add the weight of their words, ensuring that great events lead to lasting benefits for the people.

John replied in the words of Isaiah the prophet, "I am the voice of one
calling in the wilderness, 'Make straight the way for the Lord.'"
JOHN 1:23

Leadership Is Sacrifice

Leadership means getting in front and asking others to join,
rather than getting behind, kicking people from the rear,
and telling them what they should be doing.

MIKE HUCKABEE

The prophet Hosea was a spiritual leader in the Old Testament. His marriage to an adulterous woman symbolizes God's relationship with wayward Israel. Hosea's wife left him to commit sin with other men, just as Israel abandoned God to follow false gods. When Hosea found his wife, he forgave her and brought her back home—just as the Lord brought the wandering nation Israel back to Himself.

In *The Maxwell Leadership Bible*, John Maxwell describes Hosea as an example of unselfish leadership. "Hosea made several sacrifices in his leadership," Maxwell writes. At God's direction, Hosea married a prostitute, a woman with a track record of unfaithfulness. God also asked Hosea to take an unpopular message to an openly hostile, rebellious people—and Hosea unselfishly obeyed.

As Maxwell points out, "Leaders lose their right to selfishness. They must take into account the lives of others when making decisions. They must say what the people need to hear, not merely what they want to hear.... Could this explain why we have so few good leaders?"[99]

Any so-called leader who is self-seeking and self-centered is just a boss. Leadership is sacrifice. Leaders must be unselfish.

Do nothing out of selfish ambition or vain conceit. Rather, in humility
value others above yourselves, not looking to your own interests
but each of you to the interests of the others.

PHILIPPIANS 2:3–4

The Principle of Disruptive Innovation

Whenever you do a thing, act as if all the world were watching.
THOMAS JEFFERSON

In 2002, most pet foods consisted of meat trimmings, feed grains, eggshells, and bones. Lucy Postins changed that by founding The Honest Kitchen to provide human-grade pet foods.

The Honest Kitchen makes foods from "ethically raised" beef, chicken, turkey, and haddock. Food colors come from natural ingredients—spinach, carrots, and cranberries. Striking a blow against puppy mills, Postins won't distribute her foods to stores that sell puppies.

Lucy Postins calls her business model "disruptive innovation." She told *Fast Company* magazine that disruptive innovation is "creating something that consumers didn't realize they needed; it's developing a product that changes the status quo." By creating an "ethical pet food," she teaches consumers about ethical concerns inherent in most other pet foods. The act of putting these innovative pet foods on the market disrupts the assumptions—and raises the consciousness—of the consumer.

"We're a company of animal lovers," Postins says, "making products we believe in that are good enough for our own pets to eat. . . . Our products are made in a human food facility on the exact same equipment used to produce various foods people eat. . . . My staff and I really put the animals first—pets before profits—on every level."[100]

How might you adopt the principle of "disruptive innovation" to have an impact in your marketplace, field of ministry, our leadership arena?

To do what is right and just is more acceptable to the LORD than sacrifice.
PROVERBS 21:3

Great Leaders Work Harder

*You can't ask your troops to walk on water for you
if you choose to ride the Queen Mary.*
Victor Kiam

Broadcaster Art Linkletter once told me, "I first met Walt Disney in 1940 at a press conference for his movie *Fantasia*. I arrived early and found a man setting up chairs in an empty room. I said, 'When will Mr. Disney arrive?' He said, 'I'm Walt Disney.' That's Walt for you—he didn't just give orders. He worked hard."

Another Disney insight: In the wee hours before Disneyland opened, Walt was in the *20,000 Leagues Under the Sea* exhibit, spray-painting the backdrop behind the giant squid. Walt never asked his people to do anything he wasn't willing to do himself.

Retired coach Don Shula holds the NFL record for most career wins, with 347. He coached the Miami Dolphins to two Super Bowl championships and the NFL's only perfect season. Shula believed that, in a tight game between two evenly matched teams, the better-conditioned team would win.

Don Shula capped his grueling practices with sideline-to-sideline sprints called *gassers*. To motivate his players, Shula ran with them. As his son David said at Don's Hall of Fame induction in 1997, "Don Shula lives by his word. He would not ask his players to do something he would not do himself, so he ran gassers after practice with his team."[101]

Great leaders don't just bark orders. They set an example by working harder than anyone else.

*I worked harder than all of them—yet not I,
but the grace of God that was with me.*
1 Corinthians 15:10

Neither Weak Nor Wobbly

Only those leaders who act boldly in times of crisis and change are willingly followed.
JIM KOUZES

Ron Willingham is a speaker, trainer, and author in the business success field. In his book *The People Principle*, he writes about the critical importance of making bold, firm decisions.

"Decisiveness is the ability to assess situations, analyze alternatives, and move toward goal solutions. Decisiveness often results from good instincts and the willingness to run risks. It develops as you learn to trust your judgments and inclinations.

"Effective decision makers get all the facts and then take action. Often they must make decisions without all the facts. It's here that intuition and 'gut feel' come in.

"Napoleon Hill, author of the self-help classic *Think and Grow Rich*, studied the five hundred most financially successful people of his day. He wrote that each one had the common ability, after learning the known facts, to reach quick decisions, stick to them, and slowly change them if and when necessary.

"It's here that the strength of a person's commitment to action can actually transform an incorrect decision into a correct one. . . .

"Decisiveness is an essential component of effective leadership. People do not follow weak or wobbly decision-makers."[102]

Leaders must be bold, or they have ceased to lead. And no one follows a leader who does not lead. Decide boldly! Act boldly! Lead boldly!

> *"Watch me," [Gideon] told them. "Follow my lead. When I get to the edge of the camp, do exactly as I do."*
> JUDGES 7:17

The Elmira Express

I slept and dreamt that life was joy. I awoke and saw that life was service.
I acted and, behold, service was joy.
RABINDRANATH TAGORE

Ernie Davis was a running back for Syracuse University and the first African-American to win the Heisman Trophy. Nicknamed "The Elmira Express," Davis often faced racism and segregation in his career, yet he always responded with grace and character. After he was drafted by the Washington Redskins, he was traded to the Cleveland Browns. Davis never played in an NFL game, because he was diagnosed with acute monocytic leukemia in 1962. He died in 1963 at age twenty-three.

In *The Heisman*, Bill Pennington relates a story that reveals the serving heart of Ernie Davis. The story comes from Ernie's high school coach, Jim Flynn, who recalled a football practice during Ernie's junior year.

While Ernie and his teammates were in the locker room, suiting up for practice, a young white player, new to the team, came out with his shoulder pads on backward. The other players began teasing the boy mercilessly.

But Ernie Davis, the star of the team, went to the white player, lifted the pads, and readjusted them properly. He glared at the other players to silence them and said, "These things can be confusing. Don't be embarrassed. I did the same thing my first day here."[103]

Spoken like a true servant—and a great leader.

Dear children, let us not love with words
or speech but with actions and in truth.

1 JOHN 3:18

Conceptual Tinkering

*The most exciting part of inventing the flying machine was lying
awake in bed at night, dreaming of how exciting it would be to fly.*
Orville Wright

In *The Wright Way*, Mark Eppler explores the leadership traits that enabled Wilbur and Orville Wright to invent the airplane. One key trait was *vision.*

"Orville announced that during the night he had solved a problem regarding control of their machine. 'I was lying awake last night,' Orville said, 'and I studied out a new vertical, movable rudder to replace the fixed rudder we have used.' . . . Their ability to 'see' things in their heads before they tangibly existed was one of their greatest assets. I call it conceptual tinkering. . . .

"Orville. . .had a well-defined mental picture of future success. After Orville made his historic first flight, a reporter asked him if he was excited the night before the event. Orville responded that he was not. . . . He had already flown so many times in his mind that when it finally occurred, it was just another flight! . . . He had lived with that vision of success for so long that it had become reality in his mind."[104]

Call it conceptual tinkering or meditation or visioneering—great leaders take time to let their creative thoughts roam free. That's where vision comes from.

*Those who hope in the Lord will renew their strength.
They will soar on wings like eagles; they will run
and not grow weary, they will walk and not be faint.*

Isaiah 40:31

Coach K on Leadership and Communication

I have a rule on my team: When we talk to one another,
we look each other right in the eye, because I think it's tough
to lie to somebody. You give respect to somebody.

MIKE KRZYZEWSKI

Coach Mike Krzyzewski (Coach K) has coached Duke University men's basketball since 1980. At the time of this writing, he has led the Duke Blue Devils to four NCAA Championships and eleven Final Fours. He has also coached the USA men's basketball team to gold medals at the 2008 and 2012 Summer Olympics.

Coach K shared his views on leadership and communication with *SportsBusiness Journal*. Here are some insightful excerpts:

• "Even when things are going right, I still think things can go wrong. I'm always, as a leader, not being pessimistic, but watching everything so that what you think is going right, will end up right."

• "Leadership evolves. It's constantly evolving. For any leader, it has to constantly evolve because society is evolving."

• "When I first started [with USA Basketball], people would say, 'You've won three national championships, you're in the Hall of Fame. You know it.' No, you don't. There's always something to learn. To think otherwise would be arrogant and narrow-minded, and not very smart."

• "[Young players are] harder to teach than they used to be. They're different to teach. They're very visual, there's not as much face-to-face talking, they don't listen for long. We have to connect with them differently."

What are you doing to coach, teach, and influence the next generation?

Similarly, encourage the young men to be self-controlled.
TITUS 2:6

To Lead 'Em, You've Got to Love 'Em

*Great leaders genuinely care for and love the people they lead
more than they love leading itself. Leadership without love
degenerates into self-serving manipulation.*

RICK WARREN

The ability to sincerely love people, including people you've never met, is the single most important people skill a leader should have.

I saw this kind of love in action in August 1997, during an RDV Sports meeting in Grand Rapids, Michigan. Orlando Magic owner Rich DeVos, who was recovering from heart transplant surgery in London, joined the meeting via teleconferencing. Though he had just been through the most serious and delicate surgical procedure imaginable, he was cheerful and energetic, and his personal warmth dominated the room.

First item on the agenda: We needed to downsize our Magic Fan Attic team store. That meant the elimination of sixteen jobs. After about twenty minutes of discussion, Rich said, "This funeral has gone on long enough. It's time for the burial. The question is: What happens to those sixteen employees? We need to take care of them—either relocate them in the organization, or give them adequate severance pay, or help them find jobs. But I want them to be taken care of, understood?"

We understood. Rich didn't know any of those employees personally, yet he loved them. He cared about them and their families, because they had been part of his team. To lead 'em, you've got to love 'em.

Love must be sincere. Hate what is evil; cling to what is good.

ROMANS 12:9

Support Leaders Who Tell the Truth

People like being lied to. They just don't like finding out they've been lied to.
BARNEY STINSON, ON *HOW I MET YOUR MOTHER*

After the Civil War, President Lincoln delivered his Second Inaugural Address, somberly suggesting that the war may have been a divine judgment for slavery. It was also a generous speech, calling all Americans to show "malice toward none" and "charity for all" and to "bind up the nation's wounds." Lincoln knew the speech was unpopular in some quarters, yet it was a truth that needed to be told.

Terry Newell, founder of Leadership for a Responsible Society, commented on Lincoln's speech, noting that it would be hard for a president today to tell the people "a truth they do not want to hear, especially one that puts them at fault and asks of them a sacrifice."

Newell writes that when Americans vote, "they demand integrity. They should. It is an essential ingredient of leadership character." Yet those same voters often punish a president for telling the truth about the issues and challenges we face. Fearing voter retaliation, many politicians avoid hard choices.

It's not enough that the president be a leader of character, Newell concludes. "Character in the people is equally necessary. . . . It's time to give our presidents some help. It's not just about their character; it's about ours."[105]

> *Therefore say to them, "This is the nation that has not obeyed the LORD its God or responded to correction. Truth has perished; it has vanished from their lips."*
> JEREMIAH 7:28

Competence Precedes Confidence

*We gain strength, courage, and confidence by each experience
in which we really stop to look fear in the face.*
ELEANOR ROOSEVELT

Cheryl Dahle is the founder of Future of Fish, a nonprofit organization focused on problems affecting the seafood supply chain. She also leads confidence-building workshops, as she described in *Fast Company* magazine.

"I say, 'Okay, I'm going to make you a deal. I'm not going to promise to give you more *confidence*. I'm going to promise to give you more *competence*.' … Then I ask how many of them think of confidence as a prerequisite—how many of them will do something if they feel confident enough to attempt it." All hands go up.

"Then I ask them what they are confident about in their lives and how they got to be confident about those things. Whether it's horseback riding or shipping products or developing software code, they all got confidence by doing something over and over again. Oh, so then confidence is an aftermath, not a prerequisite? Bing, bing, bing!

"Then it hits them: They've been spending their whole lives waiting to be confident before trying something new, when they couldn't possibly be confident until they're competent."[106]

Moral: To build confidence, try new experiences, take courses, read books, and master new skills. Competence precedes confidence.

*All Scripture is breathed out by God and profitable for teaching,
for reproof, for correction, and for training in righteousness, that the
man of God may be competent, equipped for every good work.*
2 TIMOTHY 3:16–17 ESV

The Lions Tremble

The bravest are usually those who have the clearest vision of what is before them, glory and danger alike, and yet notwithstanding go out and meet it.

THUCYDIDES

George S. Patton Jr., first saw military action as an aide to General John J. "Black Jack" Pershing during the 1916 Pancho Villa expedition in Mexico. Commanding ten soldiers in three Dodge touring cars, Patton chased down Villa's henchmen, killing three—the first motorized attack in American history.

In October 1942, as Patton prepared to mobilize twenty-four thousand men for a landing near Casablanca, Morocco, he went to Walter Reed Army Hospital in Washington, DC, to visit his mentor, General Pershing. The ailing eighty-two-year-old Pershing told his protégé, "I'm happy they're sending you to the front. I like generals so bold that they're dangerous."

Patton thanked Pershing for permitting him to see action in Mexico. Then Patton knelt at Pershing's bedside and asked for his blessing. Pershing gave it. Patton kissed Pershing's hand, then stood and snapped off a salute.[107]

Two weeks later, Patton's forces landed on the beaches of Morocco and quickly captured Casablanca. The sultan of Morocco was so impressed with Patton's victory that he awarded him the Order of Ouissam Alaouite, inscribed in French with the motto, "The lions in their dens tremble at his approach."

George S. Patton Jr. was dangerously bold. How bold are you as a leader? Do the lions of opposition tremble at your approach?

Therefore, since we have such a hope, we are very bold.

2 CORINTHIANS 3:12

Humbled to Serve

Jesus didn't rebuke [his disciples] for wanting to be great.
He simply gave them an unexpected formula: Be a servant!
Damian D. "Skipper" Pitts

Jim Stuart is cofounder of Noble Purpose Partners. He once told *Fast Company* magazine how he discovered the power of servant leadership: "My classmates at Harvard Business School used to call me the Prussian General. For many years, that was my approach to leadership. Then I was hit by a series of personal tragedies and professional setbacks. My wife died. A mail-order venture I had started went bankrupt."

Humbled by these and other setbacks, Stuart agreed to direct the Florida Aquarium in Tampa. The nature of the position required him to stop acting like a Prussian general and start leading as a servant. "That situation forced me to draw on a deeper part of myself," he said. "We ended up with a team of people who were so high-performing that they could almost walk through walls."

Why was this team so resilient and creative? Servanthood. "Somewhere, amid all of my trials, I had begun to trust my colleagues as much as I trusted myself." The Prussian General had developed a serving heart.

Stuart concludes, "Leadership derives naturally from a commitment to service. You know that you're practicing servant leadership if your followers become wiser, healthier, more autonomous—and more likely to become servant leaders themselves."[108]

Though I am free and belong to no one, I have made myself
a slave to everyone, to win as many as possible.
1 Corinthians 9:19

The Question You Must Constantly Answer

Vision is nothing more than describing your organization's goals in a way that will mean something to your people and inspire them to action.
John Salka

Rick Warren is the founding pastor of Saddleback Church in Southern California, the eighth-largest church in America. Saddleback was born from Pastor Warren's vision of a church founded on five biblical purposes: worship, fellowship, discipleship, ministry, and evangelism.

He envisioned Saddleback as a church for people who had never been to church. The first sentence of the church's vision statement reads: "It is the dream of a place where the hurting, the depressed, the frustrated, and the confused can find love, acceptance, help, hope, forgiveness, guidance, and encouragement." The church held its first service on Easter 1980, and 205 people showed up. Most had never been to church before. The church has experienced phenomenal growth ever since.

Warren writes, "It's not the charisma of the leader that matters, but the vision of the leader. . . . You must constantly answer the question: Why are we here? If you don't know the answer, you can't lead. . . . I must continually clarify and communicate Saddleback's vision to everyone who walks through our doors. . . . Everyone needs to know why we are here and catch our vision."[109]

Lead with purpose. Lead with your vision.

*Give your servant a discerning heart to govern your people
and to distinguish between right and wrong.
For who is able to govern this great people of yours?*
1 Kings 3:9

The More Words, the Less Meaning

Make sure you finish speaking before your audience stops listening.
DOROTHY SARNOFF

There is a persistent myth that when Winston Churchill spoke at Harrow School in October 1941, his speech consisted entirely of: "Never give in, never give in, never, never, never, never!"

Well, he did say those words, but he said a great deal more besides. He spoke of the year Great Britain had been at war with the Nazi menace and the need to face the "overwhelming might of the enemy" with unyielding courage and perseverance.

He closed with these words of motivation and encouragement: "These are not dark days; these are great days—the greatest days our country has ever lived; and we must all thank God that we have been allowed, each of us according to our stations, to play a part in making these days memorable in the history of our race."

Though his speech was not as brief as is often claimed, it was quite compact, just 750 words long. Churchill understood that less can be more, and he was careful not to exhaust his listeners' attention span. He once said that public speakers wield "a power more durable than that of the great King." And Churchill wielded that power like a scalpel, not a sledgehammer.

As wise King Solomon once said, "The more the words, the less the meaning, and how does that profit anyone?" (Ecclesiastes 6:11).

> *The one who has knowledge uses words with restraint,*
> *and whoever has understanding is even-tempered.*
> PROVERBS 17:27

The Player at the End of the Bench

You can easily judge the character of a man by how
he treats those who can do nothing for him.
Johann Wolfgang von Goethe

Broadcaster Ernie Harwell recalls an incident from the career of Sparky Anderson, who managed the Cincinnati Reds and Detroit Tigers.

"When Sparky's Reds played the Orioles in the 1970 World Series, he had a second-string catcher named Pat Corrales. In his third year of backing up Johnny Bench, Corrales was finishing the sixth year of his nine-year, undistinguished career."

The Reds had lost three of four games in the series, and trailed 9–3 in the ninth inning of game five. After Orioles pitcher Mike Cuellar retired two Reds batters, the handwriting was on the wall.

"Corrales was watching from the dugout," Harwell writes. "It was his first World Series and his last." So Sparky sent Corrales into the game.

"Corrales grounded out to third baseman Brooks Robinson and the series was over. But he had batted in a World Series—thanks to a thoughtful manager."[110]

Who is the second-stringer in your organization—the backup sitting at the end of the bench? Doesn't that person deserve one at-bat in the big game?

God has put the body together, giving greater honor to the parts that lacked it,
so that there should be no division in the body, but that its parts should have
equal concern for each other. If one part suffers, every part suffers with it;
if one part is honored, every part rejoices with it.
1 Corinthians 12:24–26

Honesty: The Best Leadership Policy

*I am not bound to win, but I am bound to be true. I am not bound
to succeed, but I am bound to live up to what light I have.*
ABRAHAM LINCOLN

On June 25, 1999, the San Antonio Spurs defeated the New York Knicks in the NBA finals and won the franchise's first NBA championship. In September that year, the Spurs went to the White House to be congratulated by President Clinton. The president shook hands with each player and posed for photographs—then he checked his watch, said he had another appointment, and abruptly left.

One of the president's aides took the Spurs on a White House tour. Reaching the Oval Office, the players looked out the window and saw President Clinton out on the lawn, engaged in his "appointment." He was chipping golf balls with a nine iron.[111]

As president, Bill Clinton displayed many leadership abilities. His people skills and communication skills were among the best of any president in history. Like Ronald Reagan, he had an uncanny knack for working amicably with political opponents and getting things done for the American people.

Mr. Clinton has many excellent leadership traits—but honesty is not one of them. Had he developed the character trait of honesty, he would not have had the stain of impeachment on his legacy.

Honesty is still the best policy for leaders. What steps can you take today to strengthen your integrity and maintain your leadership legacy?

*Do not lie to each other, since you have taken
off your old self with its practices.*
COLOSSIANS 3:9

The Competency of Compromise

*Determine that the thing can and shall be done
and then we shall find the way.*
ABRAHAM LINCOLN

John Coleman is CEO of the VIA Agency in Portland, Maine. Following a contentious national election, he wrote a thoughtful piece about the leadership competency of compromise. His insights apply to any leadership arena.

"We are not governed by monarchies, despots, or militaries, but by our fellow citizens," Coleman writes, "and now our expectation is that they...will address the challenges of the day with real action. Yet recent years have created a vitriolic cesspool of inefficiency in our nation's capital.

"It takes a broad range of thinking and understanding to create the solutions for today's wildly complex world. A melding of the best ideas requires politicians of character who are wise enough to understand that compromise is not a sign of weakness but of intellect.... The greatest leaders of all time were geniuses at the art of compromise: Lincoln, FDR, Reagan, and Clinton....

"We are a melting pot of a nation that has always believed together we can accomplish anything.... American nobility comes not from privilege, but from competence. And the truly competent people are smart and secure enough to find compromises that...recognize that we are not all the same, but we all deserve consideration."[112]

Have you mastered the competency of compromise?

"Do not stop him," Jesus said. "For...whoever is not against us is for us."
MARK 9:39–40

The Three Snake Rule

Kill the snake of doubt in your soul.
KATE SEREDY

Mississippi-born Jim Barksdale was CEO of Netscape Communications from 1995 until 1999, when the company merged with AOL. During a Netscape management retreat, Barksdale formulated what came to be known as The Three Snake Rule—a handy, easy-to-remember guide to bold decision-making.

"The first rule: If you see a snake, kill it. Don't set up a snake committee. Don't set up a snake user group. Don't write snake memos. Kill it.

"The second rule: Don't play with dead snakes. (Don't revisit decisions.)

"The paradoxical third rule: All opportunities start out looking like snakes."[113]

Thomas Watson Jr., the second president of IBM, once made a statement that could serve as a commentary on The Three Snake Rule: "I never varied from the managerial rule that the worst possible thing we could do would be to lie dead in the water with any problem. Solve it, solve it quickly, solve it right or wrong. If you solved it wrong, it would come back and slap you in the face and then you could solve it right. Doing nothing is a comfortable alternative because it is without immediate risk, but it is an absolutely fatal way to manage a business."[114]

You will tread on the lion and the cobra; you will trample the great lion and the serpent. "Because he loves me," says the LORD, "I will rescue him; I will protect him, for he acknowledges my name."

PSALM 91:13–14

"You're Going to Solve It"

Show me your hands. Do they have scars from giving?
Show me your feet. Are they wounded in service?
FULTON J. SHEEN

The hospital was plagued by mismanagement and violence. A suicidal patient hanged herself in a toilet stall. A patient strangled a doctor to death. Nurses routinely ignored doctors' orders. A grand jury found that the hospital was losing a million dollars a month and described management as "a shambles."

That was the state of the Alameda County Medical Center in Oakland, California, when Wright L. Lassiter III stepped in as CEO. Lassiter approached the job with the heart of a servant. His father, a professor of business ethics, told an interviewer he had raised his son "to be a good servant leader" who works "for the greater good."

Lassiter began by dividing his top managers into teams and giving them sixteen weeks to find $21 million in budget cuts. "It's up to you," he said. "You're going to solve it." They rose to the challenge. For example, they found they could replace a $96.50 test kit with a reliable technique costing twenty-nine cents. Annual savings: more than $300,000.

Fast Company magazine observed that Lassiter "turned a shockingly mismanaged urban safety-net hospital system in one of America's most violent cities into a model for other public hospitals."[115]

And he did it with the power of servant leadership.

"I needed clothes and you clothed me, I was sick and you looked after me,
I was in prison and you came to visit me."
MATTHEW 25:36

Sometimes, the Best Vision Is Tunnel Vision

My responsibility as a leader was always to sell the vision
of being the best you could be in our trade.
DICK VERMEIL

Dick Vermeil coached the Philadelphia Eagles, St. Louis Rams, and Kansas City Chiefs. At each franchise, he took over a team with a losing record and got them into the playoffs within three seasons.

The key to Vermeil's success: hard work and vision. His vision for a championship inspired maximum effort from his coaches and players. Dick Vermeil's vision was truly a kind of *tunnel vision* that blocked all distractions.

During his first Eagles training camp, Vermeil and his assistants were watching game film. The date: July 4, 1976. About dusk, their concentration was shattered by the sound of explosions and loud whistles. Vermeil jumped to his feet and said, "What the heck is that?"

"Fireworks," one of his assistants replied, "at the college stadium."

"Fireworks? What for?"

"It's the Fourth of July, the Bicentennial—America's two-hundredth birthday."

"I don't care whose birthday it is," Vermeil said. "Tell 'em to keep it down!"

Dick Vermeil was so intensely committed to his vision that he was oblivious to America's biggest birthday party.

A powerful vision screens out distractions. Great leaders achieve great things because their minds and energies are totally focused on their vision.

We fix our eyes not on what is seen, but on what is unseen,
since what is seen is temporary, but what is unseen is eternal.
2 CORINTHIANS 4:18

Amazed at His Words

Speak well, change the world.
RANDY RIDENOUR

Jesus began His preaching ministry in the synagogues around Galilee. In His hometown of Nazareth, all who heard Jesus "spoke well of him and were amazed at the gracious words that came from his lips" (Luke 4:22).

John MacArthur, pastor of Grace Community Church in California, observes that the hearers of Jesus were "struck by His ability to communicate. Powerful orators have always been able to captivate people.... These people had just heard the greatest speaker who ever lived....

"The people were stunned at His ability to speak because they had never heard Him teach or preach before, even though He had grown up in their midst. And when He did, they were in awe. He was the greatest communicator who ever opened His mouth, possessing impeccable and consummate understanding of truth, pure and holy passion for the truth, flawless reasoning, accurate interpretation, and unmatched dexterity with the language....

"Jesus astonished them. No one would have said what the critics of Paul said: 'His presence is unimpressive and his speech contemptible.' Just the opposite was true. Jesus was amazing in presence and speech. And they kept repeating, 'Isn't that Joseph the carpenter's son?'"[116]

With His unmatched communication ability, Jesus of Nazareth set in motion a revolution that continues to this day. What leadership goals could you achieve by maximizing your communication skills?

They were amazed at his teaching, because his words had authority.
LUKE 4:32

How Will You Be Remembered?

What people will say about you will not be about what you achieved
for yourself, but what you achieved for others. Not how big
a campfire you built, but how well you kept others warm.
JAMES M. KOUZES AND BARRY Z. POSNER

Vince Lombardi is often depicted as a harsh, demanding NFL coach. His players remember him differently. After eight seasons playing for Lombardi, Willie Wood said, "Lombardi's secret was getting along with the players. He wasn't a dictator at all, contrary to public opinion.... Vince was a beautiful father confessor, a man you could really confide in."[117]

Jerry Kramer recalls Lombardi as "a very, very sensitive man. He could tear you apart, but he also had the knack of saying or doing just the right thing to bring you back up and make you believe you could be a lot better than you really were."[118]

Willie Davis was in California in September 1970 when he learned that Coach Lombardi was dying in Washington, DC. Davis boarded a plane and arrived in time to be the last of Lombardi's former players to see him alive. Lombardi was so weak that Davis stayed for only two minutes—but those two minutes were worth the entire trip. When Lombardi died, Davis felt the loss deeply: "It was very much like how I felt when I lost my mother."[119]

How will your followers remember your leadership influence?

Remember your leaders, who spoke the word of God to you.
Consider the outcome of their way of life and imitate their faith.
HEBREWS 13:7

"A Deadly Scheme We Hatched"

To educate a man in mind and not in morals
is to educate a menace to society.
THEODORE ROOSEVELT

On April 20, 1999, two armed teenage boys entered Columbine High School in Colorado and killed twelve fellow students and a teacher, injured twenty-one others, and then killed themselves. The young gunmen were articulate and well-educated. They saw themselves as deadly agents of the Darwinian "survival of the fittest" principle. They planned to "kick natural selection up a few notches," and one wore a black T-shirt with "Natural Selection" printed in red letters.[120]

Though it's tragic that many high school graduates can't read their own diplomas, we should be equally alarmed that our schools educate students in a "values free" environment in which there is no absolute morality, no right or wrong, and no judgment of immoral choices. When students are educated in mind but not in morals, they see themselves as educated animals—and they behave as predators.

In 1989, one of the founders of "values free" education, William R. Coulson, admitted that the morally vacuous approach he advocated in the 1960s had caused students to believe that "right" is "whatever they decide," adding, "It turns out to be a deadly scheme we hatched those twenty years ago."[121]

Deadly indeed, if Columbine is any indication. What can you do today to help bring moral values and character training back into our public schools?

Start children off on the way they should go, and even
when they are old they will not turn from it.
PROVERBS 22:6

Confidence Is Contagious

When your vision is backed by competence, it is exciting,
contagious, and can achieve wondrous results.
SHEILA BETHEL

In December 2009, as I prepared to fly to Detroit for a book tour, the weather reports were ominous: snow, wind, and sub-freezing temperatures. I nervously dreaded the trip.

At the terminal, I saw a Delta pilot in uniform. I asked where he was going. "Detroit," he said. It turned out he was the pilot for my flight. I told him I was nervous about the weather.

"Oh, we won't have any problems," he said. "It may get a little bumpy, but nothing too bad. The navigation equipment we have on our Delta jets is light-years beyond anything we had when I was a navy pilot. The only problem you're likely to have is when we get on the ground in Detroit—driving in that weather can be dangerous. Enjoy your flight."

I boarded the plane and we took off. Once in the air, I read a newspaper and caught a short nap. My flight reached Detroit twenty minutes early. And the pilot was right—the icy streets in Detroit were the scariest part of my trip.

The point is that *competence* is an essential component of leadership. When you are good at what you do, you radiate confidence. And confidence is contagious—it spreads to everyone around you. Competence breeds confidence. So lead with your competence, and you will lead a confident organization.

I can do all this through him who gives me strength.
PHILIPPIANS 4:13

Leadership Lessons from a Starship Captain

Risk is our business. That's what this starship is all about.
That's why we're aboard her.
CAPTAIN JAMES T. KIRK, *STAR TREK*

I'm not a *Star Trek* fan, but a friend shared these leadership insights from James Tiberius Kirk, captain of the Starship *Enterprise*.

No armchair leader, Captain Kirk beamed down to the planet, phaser in hand, like General Ridgway parachuting into France with his troops. Kirk exemplified bold leadership and bold action, and he often skinned his knuckles on Klingon jaws.

In the first episode of the series, "The Corbomite Maneuver," the *Enterprise* faces an unbeatable alien opponent. Mr. Spock compares the situation to an unwinnable chess game. Kirk replies, "Not chess, Mr. Spock. Poker. Do you know the game?" Kirk proceeds to beat the aliens with a bold and daring bluff.

Here are some other examples of Kirk's leadership wisdom:

Leadership begins with bold vision. In "Mirror Mirror," Kirk tells Spock, "In every revolution, there's one man with a vision."

Leaders ultimately decide alone. In "Dagger of the Mind," Kirk tells Dr. McCoy, "One of the advantages of being a captain, Doctor, is being able to ask for advice without necessarily having to take it."

Leaders decide, even if they have only intuition to guide them. In "Obsession," Kirk observes, "Intuition, however illogical, is recognized as a command prerogative."

What is your final frontier? And how will you boldly get there?

Those who are wise will shine like the brightness of the heavens, and those who lead many to righteousness, like the stars for ever and ever.
DANIEL 12:3

The Sniper with a Servant's Heart

Sacrifice still exists everywhere, and everywhere the elect
of each generation suffers for the salvation of the rest.
HENRI-FRÉDÉRIC AMIEL

Chris Kyle was one of America's deadliest snipers. During four tours of duty in Iraq, Kyle terrorized the terrorists, prompting them to place a bounty on his head.

Returning home to Texas, Kyle wrote a bestselling book, *American Sniper*, and served fellow veterans as a peer counselor. He took returning soldiers to the gun range near his home. Shooting, he found, was good therapy for emotional battle scars.

On February 2, 2013, Kyle and a friend, Chad Littlefield, took Eddie Ray Routh, a twenty-five-year-old former marine corporal, to the gun range. What happened next is murky—but this much is clear: Routh shot and killed both men, then fled in Kyle's pickup. He was captured and charged with murder.

Travis Cox, a friend of Chris Kyle's, said Kyle "was a servant leader in helping his brothers and sisters dealing with post-traumatic stress disorder. . . . He would do anything he could to serve veterans."

Of his role as a military sniper, Kyle said, "It was my duty to shoot, and I don't regret it." His accuracy with a gun saved many American lives, and he was the recipient of two Silver Stars and five Bronze Stars for Valor.[122] Though there was a bounty on his head in Iraq, he died in Texas—a wounded healer and a servant leader.

"He trains my hands for battle; my arms can bend a bow of bronze."
2 SAMUEL 22:35

"We Will Cover the End of the World"

Vision is everything for a leader. It is utterly indispensable. Why?
Because vision leads the leader. It paints the target.
It sparks and fuels the fire within.
John Maxwell

Media mogul Ted Turner had a vision for a global twenty-four-hour news channel. Amazingly, none of the big networks had ever imagined such a thing. CBS, NBC, and ABC all had globe-spanning news divisions, and it would have been a simple matter to feed news content to an around-the-clock cable news desk. Lacking vision, the networks devoted their vast resources to producing one paltry half hour of news per night.

Ted Turner assembled his own news-gathering powerhouse, hiring as anchor the highly regarded Bernard Shaw, previously of ABC. As Turner launched Cable News Network in June 1980, he said, "We won't be signing off until the world ends. We'll be on, and we will cover the end of the world, live."[123]

Turner's visionary network still brings us the news of the world today. His vision for CNN inspired confidence—a news network so dependable that it would still be around to broadcast the Apocalypse.

As a leader, your vision should be so succinct and memorable that you could print it on a T-shirt—and you should! Share your vision with your people, and give them a goal to shoot for, a dream to work for. People who believe in a dream will pay any price to make your vision come true.

"Blessed are your eyes because they see, and your ears because they hear."
Matthew 13:16

Love Your Audience

Some people want the audience to love them. I love the audience.
LUCIANO PAVAROTTI

We easily forget that public speaking is not about the speaker. It's about the *audience*. The audience hasn't come to serve the speaker; the speaker has come to serve the audience. So we must ask ourselves: *What do our listeners need to hear?*

I once asked Jack Canfield, cofounder of the *Chicken Soup for the Soul* franchise, how he approaches audiences.

"I tell myself, 'Love your audience,'" he said. "I believe the speaker must come with a sense of purpose, wanting to give the audience a gift. If you're there only for yourself, the audience will pick up on that. If you're there to love and serve them, they will know that as well."

That's a profound insight: Love your audience. Give your audience the gift of your insight, your experience, your caring.

Business author Tom Peters once told me, "The best speakers convert one individual at a time. If there are five thousand people in your audience, you must still see them as individuals. You must become one of them and genuinely feel their pain. You've got to care about them. You've got to be real and disclose who you are as an authentic human being. Be vulnerable. People can sense that a mile away—and they respond to it."

To lead and influence people, we must love them.

If I speak in the tongues of men or of angels, but do not have love,
I am only a resounding gong or a clanging cymbal.
1 CORINTHIANS 13:1

A Meal with the Troops

The hospitality of God embodied in the table fellowship of Jesus is a celebration and sign of his grace and generosity. And we're to imitate that generosity.
Tim Chester, *A Meal with Jesus*

Leaders eat with their troops," Bob Briner writes in *Leadership Lessons of Jesus*. "Food can be a great catalyst for building relationships and for teaching."

Briner reminds us that the first recorded miracle of Jesus was turning water into wine. Later, He fed thousands from a single basket of bread and dried fish. At the Last Supper, He turned a Passover meal into a Christian sacrament. On the day of His resurrection, Jesus dined with two disciples—and only when He broke the bread did they recognize Him. Days later, Jesus prepared His disciples a breakfast of grilled fish.

Sharing a meal with someone is an act of affirmation. It says, "I like you. I enjoy being with you." Throughout the Gospels, Jesus used shared meals to build relationships with His disciples.

Bob Briner concludes, "Leaders do not neglect the power of food and mealtimes to set the stage for building lasting, productive relationships and imparting important lessons. . . . Nothing breaks down barriers like sharing a Coke and a hamburger or a quick breakfast together. . . . The wise leader will be sure to 'break bread' occasionally with those he seeks to lead."[124]

Jesus declared, "I am the bread of life. Whoever comes to me will never go hungry, and whoever believes in me will never be thirsty."
John 6:35

Great Leaders Keep Soldiering On

I'll never retire. I'm just using up somebody else's oxygen if I retire.
SAM PHILLIPS

In late 2012, I interviewed author Tullian Tchividjian on my radio show. He is senior pastor of Coral Ridge Presbyterian Church in Ft. Lauderdale, Florida, and a grandson of evangelist Billy Graham.

I asked about his ninety-four-year-old grandfather. "Daddy Bill is physically frail," Tchividjian said, "but he's very engaged with life, and still has books he wants to write. He doesn't fear death, but he was never prepared to get old. It kind of snuck up on him. But he still wants to make a difference with his life."

I thought, *Wow! A genuine leader never retires. He perseveres to his last breath.*

Billy Graham reminds me of Caleb, the Old Testament hero, a leader in the conquest of the Promised Land. When Caleb was eighty-five, well past "retirement age," Joshua divided the land among the tribes. Yet Caleb didn't ask for a retirement villa—he asked for a *challenge.* "Give me a sword and another hill to climb!" he said.

Like Billy Graham and Caleb, keep leading, keep soldiering, keep fighting the good fight. As long as there is work to do, be a leader.

> *[Caleb said:] "So here I am today, eighty-five years old!*
> *I am still as strong today as the day Moses sent me out;*
> *I'm just as vigorous to go out to battle now as I was then.*
> *Now give me this hill country that the LORD promised me that day."*
> JOSHUA 14:10–12

Competent Leadership Inspires Trust

The mark of a good leader is loyal followers;
leadership is nothing without a following.
PROVERBS 14:28 MSG

In 1803, the United States, at the behest of President Thomas Jefferson, acquired 827,000 square miles of land known as the Louisiana Purchase. Jefferson commissioned explorers Meriwether Lewis and William Clark to map this new frontier. Lewis and Clark led thirty-one frontiersmen on an expedition to trace the course of the Missouri River and seek a waterway to the Pacific Ocean.

In June 1805, in present-day Montana, Lewis and Clark reached a fork in the river. Should they take the left branch or the right? Which was the Missouri River and which was a mere tributary? Lewis and Clark believed the left fork was the true Missouri; their companions believed it was the right.

Yet Lewis and Clark had gained such a reputation for competence that (as Meriwether Lewis wrote in his journal) the men "were ready to follow us any wher [sic] we thought proper to direct but that they still thought that the other was the river."[125] After ten days following the left fork, they reached the Great Falls— proof that Lewis and Clark were on the correct path.

Lewis and Clark's followers all thought their leaders were wrong but followed them anyway. That's how much confidence they had in the competence of Meriwether Lewis and William Clark. Competent leaders inspire committed followership.

Does your leadership competence inspire such trust?

A large population is a king's glory, but without subjects a prince is ruined.
PROVERBS 14:28

Something Worth Dying For

There can be no courage unless you're scared.
Eddie Rickenbacker

Donald T. Phillips tells a story about the boldly courageous leadership of Dr. Martin Luther King Jr. The incident took place during a civil rights demonstration in Selma, Alabama.

"As [Dr. King's] group of protesters approached the Selma courthouse," Phillips writes, "they were met by more than three hundred angry white segregationists. Fearing for Martin's safety, Andrew Young pulled up in a car and asked him to get in. 'No,' came the reply. 'I am going to walk.'"

Another King associate, Hosea Williams, said that Dr. King walked straight toward the mob. "Dr. King smiled," Williams recalled, "and said, 'Excuse me, please.' And the line just opened up. He walked right on up through them and got on the sidewalk. . . . And not one of them touched him."

Phillips concludes, "What is it that gives a person such courage? . . . [Dr. King's] desire to achieve the goals of the movement, coupled with the fact that he cared so deeply about what he was doing, outweighed any personal risk he might encounter."[126]

Is there a principle you love so dearly that you would dare to face an angry mob? Is there an issue that would inspire you to boldly place your life on the line? A leader who has something worth dying for has everything to live for.

> *Even though I walk through the valley of the shadow of death,*
> *I will fear no evil, for you are with me.*
> Psalm 23:4 esv

Servants First

I had to admire him as a good and perfect servant.
He walked along the lanes in front of me, nimbly and patiently,
indicating the way; he was the perfect guide.
HERMANN HESSE, *THE JOURNEY TO THE EAST*

Servant leadership was invented by Jesus of Nazareth, who said, "Anyone who wants to be first must be the very last, and the servant of all" (Mark 9:35). Robert Greenleaf coined the term *servant leader* in his 1970 essay "The Servant as Leader."

Greenleaf was inspired by Hermann Hesse's 1932 novel *The Journey to the East*, the tale of a pilgrimage taken by a group of poets and artists. Among them is a servant, Leo, who does menial chores. When Leo disappears, the entire group experiences "a feeling of impending disaster and menacing destiny."[127]

Leo's disappearance devastates the group, *because the servant is the leader*. Without the humble, selfless servant, the group loses cohesion and coherence. As Robert Greenleaf observes, "This story clearly says that *the great leader is seen as servant first*, and that simple fact is the key to his greatness. Leo was actually the leader all of the time, but he was servant first because that was what he was, *deep down inside*."[128]

As servant leaders, we're called to be servants first—not bosses who sometimes serve, but out-and-out servants, self-effacing and self-sacrificing, who serve by leading and lead by serving. Only when we grasp this paradoxical truth do we authentically lead.

Carry each other's burdens, and in this way you will fulfill the law of Christ.
GALATIANS 6:2

A Shared Vision

*The greatest leaders mobilize others by coalescing
people around a shared vision.*
KENNETH BLANCHARD

In *A Leader's Legacy*, James M. Kouzes and Barry Z. Posner observe that many leaders have the mistaken notion that they should be lonely visionaries. "If others expected them to be forward-looking," the authors write, "then they had to go off all alone into the wilderness, climb to the top of some mountain," and receive a vision in the form of a revelation.[129] But leaders are not expected to be prophets.

"What people really want to hear," Kouzes and Posner conclude, "is not the leader's vision. They want to hear about *their own* aspirations. They want to hear how their dreams will come true and their hopes will be fulfilled. They want to see themselves in the picture of the future that the leader is painting. The very best leaders understand that their key task is inspiring a *shared* vision."[130]

It's true. The people in your organization will not be inspired by a "vision" made up of nothing but your own personal ambitions. They want to know how the fulfillment of that vision will benefit *them*.

Consider bringing your people together for a shared vision-casting celebration. Encourage wide-open imagination, spontaneity, and creativity. Let people know that their ideas and dreams are valued. People buy into what benefits them. And if they buy in, they will build the dream they share with you.

There is surely a future hope for you, and your hope will not be cut off.
PROVERBS 23:18

Notes from the Communicator in Chief

*I wasn't a great communicator, but I communicated great things,
and they didn't spring full bloom from my brow,
they came from the heart of a great nation.*
RONALD REAGAN

Michael Reagan, the elder son of President Ronald Reagan, was a guest on my radio show. He told me how, at the 1976 Republican convention, President Ford beckoned from the platform and invited his primary rival to say a few words.

When Ronald and Nancy Reagan joined the president and Mrs. Ford on the platform, Reagan whispered to Nancy, "I don't know what to say!"

Then he stepped to the microphone and delivered one of the most eloquent speeches of his career. Delegates wept as they listened—and that five-minute speech laid the groundwork for Reagan's election as president four years later.

Where did that speech come from? Answer: Reagan had years of public speaking experience. He had spent ten years as a spokesman for General Electric, touring the country, delivering up to a dozen speeches per day.

Michael Reagan recalls seeing bundles of three-by-five cards his father had handwritten, bound with rubber bands, and sorted by topic. Reagan's GE years were the best training a leader could have. "My father was not just the commander in chief," Michael concluded. "He was the communicator in chief."

Accept every opportunity to speak, and build your communicating confidence and mastery through experience.

*The LORD was with Samuel as he grew up,
and he let none of Samuel's words fall to the ground.*
1 SAMUEL 3:19

It Costs Nothing and Means Everything

*If you remember anything else from me, remember this. It really doesn't
cost anything to be nice, and the rewards can be unimaginable.*
Paul "Bear" Bryant

Franklin D. Roosevelt contracted polio in 1921, at age thirty-nine. The illness
left him paralyzed from the waist down, though his disability was kept from
public view.

After Roosevelt became president, the Chrysler Corporation built a hand-
controlled car for him. Designer W. F. Chamberlain delivered it to the White
House. Chamberlain later recalled, "I taught President Roosevelt how to handle
a car with a lot of unusual gadgets, but he taught me a lot about the fine art of
handling people....

"He called me by name, made me feel very comfortable, and particularly impressed me with the fact that he was vitally interested in things I had to show him.

"When Roosevelt's friends and associates admired the machine, he said in
their presence, 'Mr. Chamberlain, I certainly appreciate all the time and effort you
have spent in developing this car. It is a mighty fine job.'...

"When the driving lesson was finished, the president turned to me and said:
'Well, Mr. Chamberlain, I have been keeping the Federal Reserve Board waiting
thirty minutes. I guess I had better get back to work.'"[131]

It doesn't cost anything to show kindness and publicly praise others for a job
well done. Have you mastered the people skill of kindness?

*As God's chosen people, holy and dearly loved, clothe yourselves with
compassion, kindness, humility, gentleness, and patience.*
Colossians 3:12

The Leadership Traits of the Apostle Paul

What we learn from the apostle Paul is the same thing Jesus taught:
that character—not style, not technique, not methodology,
but character—is the true biblical test of great leadership.

JOHN MACARTHUR

In Acts 20, Paul delivers a farewell speech to the Ephesian elders—a speech that says a lot about his leadership traits:

"I served the Lord with great humility" (verse 19). Paul practiced *humble servanthood*.

"You know that I have not hesitated to preach" (verse 20). Paul faithfully *communicated* his message.

"I have declared to both Jews and Greeks that they must. . .have faith in our Lord Jesus" (verse 21). Paul was *unprejudiced* and had *compassion* for the lost.

"I am going to Jerusalem, not knowing what will happen to me there" (verse 22). Paul had great *courage and boldness* in following God's leading.

"My only aim is to finish the race" (verse 24). Paul faithfully *persevered*.

"Be shepherds of the church" (verse 28). Paul had a *shepherd's heart* for people.

"I showed you that by this kind of hard work we must help the weak, remembering the words the Lord Jesus himself said: 'It is more blessed to give than to receive'" (verse 35). Paul was *hardworking* and *generous*.

As you look at this list of leadership traits, which traits you are strong in? Which do you need to strengthen?

Follow my example, as I follow the example of Christ.
1 CORINTHIANS 11:1

Are You a Boss or a Leader?

*A competent and self-confident person is incapable of jealousy in anything.
Jealousy is invariably a symptom of neurotic insecurity.*
Robert A. Heinlein

Selfridges & Co. is an elite department store chain in Great Britain, founded in 1909 by Harry Gordon Selfridge. A master sloganeer, Selfridge originated such sayings as "The customer is always right" and "There's no fun like work." In 1923, he said the following about bosses and leaders:

"The boss drives people; the leader coaches them. The boss depends on authority; the leader on goodwill. The boss inspires fear; the leader inspires enthusiasm. The boss says 'I'; the leader says '*we*.' The boss fixes the blame for the breakdown; the leader fixes the breakdown. The boss says, '*go*'; the leader says, '*let's go*!'"[132]

Some observations of my own: Bosses take credit; leaders give credit. Bosses criticize in public; leaders praise in public. Bosses expect to be served; leaders serve others. Bosses seek power; leaders empower others. Bosses are selfish; leaders are selfless.

As the Chinese philosopher Laozi observed, "A leader is best when people barely know he exists. . . . When his work is done, his aim fulfilled, they will say: 'We did it ourselves.'"[133] Are you a boss—or a leader?

*Jesus said to them, "The kings of the Gentiles lord it over them;
and those who exercise authority over them call themselves Benefactors.
But you are not to be like that. Instead, the greatest among you should
be like the youngest, and the one who rules like the one who serves."*
Luke 22:25–26

Prepare to Be Boldly Decisive

I may act on my intuition—
but only if my hunches are supported by the facts.
Lee Iacocca

Harry Truman was widely admired as a boldly decisive president. He took office upon the death of Franklin Roosevelt in April 1945. FDR had never briefed Truman on war strategy, his meetings with Stalin and Churchill, or the development of the atomic bomb. So Truman had a lot to catch up on.

President Truman always made up his mind firmly and without second-guessing himself. Why? Preparation. Historians Henry and Richard Blackaby write that Truman "would fastidiously examine every document and briefing until he understood the issues and was thoroughly equipped to make a decision. Truman became known for his decisiveness, but this decisiveness was born of his meticulous preparation. Leaders can make momentous decisions with confidence if they are adequately prepared."[134]

Truman himself once explained, "Whenever it comes time to make a decision, I make it and forget about it, and go to work on something else…. You never have time to stop. You've got to keep going because there's always a decision just ahead of you that you've got to make, and you don't want to look back. If you make a mistake in one of these decisions, correct it by another decision, and go ahead."[135]

To be a decisive leader, gather the facts, decide the matter—and then move on.

Who, then, are those who fear the Lord?
He will instruct them in the ways they should choose.
Psalm 25:12

Servant Leader—or Self-Serving Leader?

It is a shame that so many leaders spend their time pondering their rights as leaders instead of their awesome responsibilities as leaders.
James C. Hunter, *The Servant*

Leadership icon Ken Blanchard observes that the most pervasive leadership style in the world is "seagull management," which he defines this way: "Managers might set goals and then disappear until you screw up. Then they fly in, make a lot of noise, dump on everybody, and fly out. They think that's great leadership."[136]

He often asks audiences, "How do you know whether you're doing a good job?" The top response: "Nobody has yelled at me lately." He encourages leaders to wander around, catching people in the act of doing things well, then praising them in front of their peers.

Blanchard says that great leaders are servant leaders, not self-serving leaders. "One of the quickest ways you can tell the difference between servant leaders and self-serving leaders," he writes, "is how they handle feedback, since one of the biggest fears that self-serving leaders have is losing their position. Self-serving leaders spend most of their time protecting their status. . . . Servant leaders. . .welcome feedback, viewing it as a source of useful information on how they can provide better service."[137]

To lead well, don't be a seagull. Don't be self-serving. Be a servant.

Do nothing out of selfish ambition or vain conceit. Rather, in humility value others above yourselves, not looking to your own interests but each of you to the interests of the others.
Philippians 2:3–4

Proclaim Your Vision!

You need a[n]. . .exceptionally clear vision. And to me, a vision is something that you can say in one sentence. The fewer the words the better.
RON JOHNSON

P roclaim your vision!

Highlight it whenever you speak to audiences. Print it on T-shirts and on your webpage. Post it on banners in your lobby, lunchroom, conference rooms, and washrooms. If your vision won't fit in those places, it's too long. Condense it, distill it to its essence, and make it memorable.

Former General Electric CEO Jack Welch put it this way: "You need an overarching message, something big, but simple and understandable. Whatever it is, every idea you present must be something you could get across easily at a cocktail party with strangers. If only aficionados of your industry can understand what you're saying, you've blown it."[138]

Howard Putnam, former CEO of Southwest Airlines, explains why a clear, concise vision is crucial to success: "Most companies fail in their growth because they don't have a vision. They don't know where to go. When you have a vision and someone comes to you with some convoluted idea, you can hold it up to the vision and ask, Does it fit? Does it fly? If not, don't bother me. A vision must be so strong that it can outweigh the egos of managers that might want to take off in a different direction."[139]

Keep it brief, make it unforgettable, and proclaim your vision!

"As you go, proclaim this message: 'The kingdom of heaven has come near.'"
MATTHEW 10:7

Your Signature Speech

It usually takes more than three weeks to prepare a good impromptu speech.
MARK TWAIN

To be an effective speaker, craft one signature speech that expresses the most earnest convictions of your being. Hone that message, practice it endlessly, and make it completely yours.

Your signature speech should be so unique to you that no one else in the world could deliver it. It should contain personal stories that reveal who you are and what you are passionate about. It should contain ideas and insights that your audience will never hear from anyone else.

Once you've structured your speech, rehearse it until you are able to deliver it confidently, without notes. This is your "ace-in-the-hole" speech—the go-to talk you can deliver at a moment's notice. It should be long enough to fill fifty minutes, yet flexible enough to edit on the fly (cut a few stories here, a few points there) and deliver in as little as fifteen minutes.

As you gain experience and confidence as a speaker, you'll come up with additional signature speeches on different topics. But at the beginning of your speaking career, make sure you have one great message stored in your mental circuitry.

To be a leader of influence, always be ready with a few well-chosen words.

"A good man brings good things out of the good stored up in his heart, and an evil man brings evil things out of the evil stored up in his heart. For the mouth speaks what the heart is full of."
LUKE 6:45

Lead People—Don't Try to Change Them

You can change things, but you can't change people.
DAVID IRVINE

Robert Mondavi was a leading California vintner who singlehandedly revolutionized the way wines are made and marketed. In *Harvests of Joy*, he shares some leadership wisdom he learned late in life.

"At the age of about seventy-five, I finally learned to accept the cold, hard truth: You cannot change people. Influence them a little, yes. But truly change them, no—unless they themselves deeply want to change.... This was a very difficult lesson for me to learn and accept. But once I understood that you can't change people...it is amazing what peace of mind I felt."[140]

Leadership experts Warren G. Bennis and Burt Nanus observe that great leaders achieve a level of what they call "emotional wisdom," which is expressed through certain people skills. The first of those skills, they write, is "the ability to accept people as they are, not as you would like them to be." They explain: "This can be seen as the height of wisdom—to 'enter the skin' of someone else, to understand what other people are like on *their* terms, rather than judging them."[141]

Don't wait until late in life to realize that you can't change people. Seek to influence people—but at the same time, seek to understand and accept them as they are.

Accept one another, then, just as Christ accepted you,
in order to bring praise to God.
ROMANS 15:7

Lead and Inspire by Character

You cannot lead by memo, you cannot lead by shouting, you cannot lead by delegation of your responsibility—you must lead by example.
CHARLES KRULAK

General Charles Chandler Krulak served as commandant of the US Marine Corps from 1995 to 1999. He is known in military circles for envisioning the concept known as the Three Block War. During two tours in Vietnam, he fought Vietcong guerrillas and the North Vietnamese Army and took part in the effort to "win the hearts and minds" of the Vietnamese people. He became convinced he had seen the future of warfare—a multifaceted battlefield, the Three Block War.

He said that within three city blocks, the US military should be prepared to meet a block of civilians needing aid, a block requiring peacekeeping operations, and a block of intense combat against asymmetrical (guerrilla) forces. His vision of warfare has been validated on battlefields from Iraq and Afghanistan to Somalia.

When an interviewer asked his philosophy of leadership, Krulak replied, "The most important leadership trait is to be a man or woman of *character*. . . . I define character as (1) being selfless, (2) having moral courage, and (3) having integrity. . . . Character is a choice. You choose to be a man or woman of character. Leaders are in the inspiration business and anyone who seeks to inspire must have the character to inspire."[142]

Who are you leading and inspiring with your character today?

In everything set them an example by doing what is good.
TITUS 2:7

Prepared for Adversity

A competent leader can get efficient service from poor troops, while on the contrary an incapable leader can demoralize the best of troops.
GENERAL JOHN J. "BLACK JACK" PERSHING

Former NBA star Kenny Smith played for Coach Dean Smith at the University of North Carolina. In Kenny's senior year, the Tar Heels went to Clemson ranked first in the nation, but were trailing by twenty at halftime.

"Coach gives us a little speech," Kenny recalls. "We. . .cut it to about fifteen. And he calls a timeout. He looks at us and says: 'We're right where we want to be.'

"I'm like: 'We're down fifteen. . . . We're not right where we want to be."

Coach Smith had repeatedly drilled them for situations like this one. Kenny and his teammates hadn't understood the reason for those drills—but they soon found out. Coach Smith sent them back into the game.

"We went into running our plays, running our defenses," Kenny recalls. "We did everything we had done in practice. He never called a play. He never called a timeout."

The result? "We won the game by nine."

That game taught Kenny Smith a valuable life lesson: "If I prepare myself, I can be down fifteen and still come out on top."[143]

All leaders face setbacks. If you build the right attitudes, habits, and skills into your life, you and your team will come out on top.

Commit to the LORD whatever you do, and he will establish your plans.
PROVERBS 16:3

Boldness to Stand Alone

Where the world is changing and changing fast,
your thoughts have to be bold.
ANDREA GUERRA

Throughout history, God has called leaders to take bold, lonely action: Joseph versus Potiphar's wife, Moses versus Pharaoh, David versus Goliath, and Elijah versus the prophets of Baal. God called Noah to build a boat in the desert when no rain was forecast. Sooner or later, most leaders are called to boldly go where no leader has gone before.

William Taylor, cofounder of *Fast Company* magazine, says, "The true mark of a leader is the willingness to stick with a bold course of action—an unconventional business strategy, a unique product-development roadmap, a controversial marketing campaign—even as the rest of the world wonders why you're not marching in step with the status quo. In other words, real leaders are happy to zig while others zag. . . . The only way to stand out from the crowd is to stand for something special. . . .

"It's hard to overcome the pull of conventional wisdom. . . . That's why it's hard for leaders to do something genuinely new—to embrace one-of-a-kind ideas in a world filled with me-too thinking. But that's the job description for leadership today. . . .

"How are you planning to zig while everyone else zags?"[144]

Do not conform to the pattern of this world, but be transformed
by the renewing of your mind. Then you will be able to test and approve
what God's will is—his good, pleasing, and perfect will.
ROMANS 12:2

The Toughest Leader of All

When you leave this earth, you can take with you
nothing that you have received—only what you have given:
A heart enriched by honest service, love, sacrifice, and courage.

Saint Francis of Assisi

James Hunter, author of *The World's Most Powerful Leadership Principle*, started an employee relations company in the mid-1980s. He worked with organizations troubled by absenteeism, high turnover, and low morale. He observed, "The issue was leadership, every time." Whether organizations were healthy or sick, leadership got them there. Good leadership produced healthy traits; bad leadership produced bad symptoms.

Then he discovered servant leadership—and everything fell into place. But while the phrase *servant leadership* may sound warm and fuzzy, it can be rugged in practice.

"The role of the leader," Hunter says, "is to identify and meet needs. We're not here to do what people want—but we are here to do what people need. Some of the great servant leaders I have known in my career have been tough as nails when it comes to…accountability and values and doing the right thing.… They're about meeting the needs of people—the need to be appreciated, the need to be listened to, the need to be communicated with, the need to be held accountable, the need to know where the boundaries are."

A servant isn't a pushover or a weakling. A servant is the toughest leader of all.

We who are strong ought to bear with the failings
of the weak and not to please ourselves.

Romans 15:1

Shoot for the Moon!

Shoot for the moon. Even if you miss, you will still be among the stars.
Les Brown

On May 25, 1961, President John F. Kennedy committed America to a vision of "achieving the goal, before this decade is out, of landing a man on the moon and returning him safely to the earth." That vision was achieved on July 20, 1969, when Apollo 11 astronauts Neil Armstrong and Buzz Aldrin landed on the moon.

At the same time, our leaders were already shifting their focus away from the moon. In 1969, President Nixon's Space Task Group devised a plan for a small fleet of reusable space shuttles. Mr. Nixon announced the new program in January 1972.

What was his vision? The space shuttle, he said, would serve as a "space truck" for hauling cargo and repairing satellites. Public interest in space immediately began to wane.

As the *Chicago Tribune* opined in 2010, "The space shuttle flares little in the imagination these days. The fact that the fleet is scheduled to be grounded for good next year rates a shrug and a scratch of the head: Do they still fly those contraptions?"[145]

The shuttle program ended in 2011. The *Challenger* and *Columbia* tragedies didn't kill it. Budget cuts and political infighting didn't kill it. The space shuttle died due to a lack of a clear, compelling vision for the future.

As you formulate your leadership vision, don't try to inspire people with a "truck." Shoot for the moon!

Praise him, sun and moon; praise him, all you shining stars.
Psalm 148:3

A Conversation with Your Audience

*Every time you have a conversation you are speaking without notes.
So you know you can do it.*
GEORGE TOROK

When author Ray Bradbury first began giving speeches in 1948, he lectured from prepared notes. During one early talk, he looked up from his notes and saw that his audience was half-asleep. So he gave a shout, threw his notes on the floor, and stomped on them. His audience instantly awoke! Bradbury continued his talk, speaking straight from the heart—and he never used notes again.

To be confident, speak from the heart, not from notecards. You may think, "How can I give a speech without notes? Do I memorize it word for word?" No! People don't want to hear you recite from memory. They want a conversation with you.

Organize your talk—your stories and key points. Learn the structure of your talk. Practice it repeatedly. Follow your outline, speak from your heart, have a conversation. You'll know the flow of your message, but the exact wording will be different every time you give it.

With practice, you'll gain the confidence to converse with your audience—*without notes and without fear*. You'll go from stage fright to total confidence, stepping onto the stage with nothing between you and your audience. Believe me, when you speak without notes, you'll have their attention. They'll sit up straight and lean forward.

And you'll have 'em in the palm of your hand.

"Now go; I will help you speak and will teach you what to say."
EXODUS 4:12

Are You Too Busy to Lead People?

Beware the barrenness of a busy life.
SOCRATES

Julia Ward Howe was a prominent abolitionist in America, and the author of "The Battle Hymn of the Republic." Mrs. Howe once asked Senator Charles Sumner of Massachusetts to lend help to a needy family.

"I'm sorry, Mrs. Howe, but I can't," the senator replied. "I've become so busy that I can no longer devote any time to individuals."

Mrs. Howe replied, "Not even God is that busy!"

One of the most important of all people skills is the ability to take time for individuals. Two presidents from opposite ends of the spectrum were famed for taking time to help people with their problems.

Many who wrote to President Reagan received handwritten replies from the president himself. When people wrote him about their financial problems, he sometimes sent them a check from his personal bank account.

President Clinton was known for meeting people, asking for their stories, listening attentively, and remembering them by name even months or years later.

Jesus was never too busy for individuals. The Gospels contain many accounts of His one-on-one ministry with individuals. Great leaders understand that they lead *people*, not programs. If we're too busy for people, we're too busy, period.

[Bartimaeus] began to shout, "Jesus, Son of David, have mercy on me!"
Many rebuked him and told him to be quiet, but he shouted all the more,
"Son of David, have mercy on me!" Jesus stopped and said, "Call him."
MARK 10:47–49

The Making of a Chief

Character is the indispensable foundation upon which good leadership is built.
STEVE FORBES

Murray Coleman of *Investor's Business Daily* interviewed Ron His Horse Is Thunder, a great-great-great grandson of Lakota Sioux warrior Sitting Bull. The Sioux scion told Coleman the story of how Sitting Bull became chief.

Two rivals—Sitting Bull and another warrior—vied for the leadership of the tribe. The tribal elders devised a plan to reveal the character of each man. They sent a handsome young warrior to Sitting Bull's rival with a message: "Your wife is now with me." Wife-stealing was one of the worst crimes imaginable under Sioux custom.

The rival became enraged, grabbed his gun, and chased the young warrior through the camp. Fortunately, the elders halted the chase before anyone got hurt.

The young warrior then went to Sitting Bull with the same message. Instead of becoming enraged, Sitting Bull offered the young man his horse and blankets, so that his wife would be well cared for.

Coleman explains, "The tribe's elders saw that Sitting Bull put his jealousy aside to maintain harmony in the camp—and put his wife's welfare above his own. As a result, Sitting Bull's stature grew and he became chief."

Murray Coleman concludes, "The measure of a leader is character."[146] Authentic leaders put the interests of the community ahead of their own.

The fruit of the Spirit is love, joy, peace, forbearance, kindness, goodness, faithfulness, gentleness, and self-control. Against such things there is no law.
GALATIANS 5:22–23

The Leader on the Path

*Pass on what you heard from me. . .to reliable
leaders who are competent to teach others.*
2 TIMOTHY 2:2 MSG

David Egner shares a leadership insight he learned while walking with Whitaker, his dog: "Whitaker and I like to take early-morning walks through the woods. He runs ahead while I amble along, meditating or praying. I know where we're going; he's not sure. I stay on the trail and he trots ahead—sniffing, investigating, and taking occasional forays into the forest. . . .

"Though Whit is ahead, I'm leading. Every so often he checks to see where I am. If I've turned back toward home or gone on to another trail, I hear his pounding feet and panting breath as he races to catch up. . . . Then we walk the trail together again."

Great leaders choose the path and know the way, but they give their followers freedom to explore and make decisions, to move out ahead or race to catch up. We don't want our followers to trudge behind us, single file. We want followers who are curious and excited about the journey.

Whether your followers trot ahead or lag behind, they'll always come back because you're the leader, the mentor, the visionary. They look to you because you know the path—and you are competent to lead and to teach.

*I myself am convinced, my brothers and sisters, that you yourselves are full
of goodness, filled with knowledge and competent to instruct one another.*
ROMANS 15:14

Encourage Bold Decisions—
and Forgive Mistakes

*Without mistakes, innovation in business is virtually impossible. Ideas become
great programs and products because of trial and error.*
M. DAVID DEALY

James E. Burke worked for Johnson & Johnson for four decades and was CEO
from 1976 to 1989. He tells a story that reveals the bold leadership philosophy
of longtime J&J leader General Robert Wood Johnson II.

"I once developed a new product that failed badly, and General Johnson
called me in, and I was sure he was going to fire me. . . . Johnson said to me, 'I understand you lost over one million dollars.' And I said, 'Yes, sir. That is correct.' . . .

"He stood up and held out his hand. He said, 'I just want to congratulate
you. All business is making decisions, and if you don't make decisions, you won't
have any failures. The hardest job I have is getting people to make decisions. If you
make that same decision wrong again, I'll fire you. But I hope you'll make a lot of
others, and that you will understand that there are going to be more failures than
successes.'"

Burke concludes, "If you believe that growth comes from risk taking, that
you cannot grow without it, then it is essential in leading people toward growth
to get them to make decisions—and to make mistakes."

Great leaders encourage followers to make bold decisions.

*If we confess our sins, he is faithful and just and will forgive
us our sins and purify us from all unrighteousness.*

1 JOHN 1:9

Resolve Conflict through Serving

An element of conflict in every discussion is a very good thing.
It shows that everyone is taking part and no one is left out.
Elwood P. Dowd, in *Harvey*

The New Testament talks a lot about conflict. In Philippians 4:2, Paul steps between Euodia and Syntyche, two battling women in the Philippian church. And Paul urges the Ephesians, "Make every effort to keep the unity of the Spirit through the bond of peace" (Ephesians 4:3).

You cannot avoid, ignore, or suppress conflict. Because conflict is inevitable, managing conflict is a big part of the job description of any leader. Well-managed conflict can lead to growth and new ideas—but mismanaged conflict can destroy your organization. Here are some ways to manage conflict for the good of your organization:

1. *Welcome disagreements.* Ask for ideas and opinions, drop your defenses, and encourage people to speak candidly.

2. *Keep your cool.* When others lose their temper, keep yours. When others shout, lower your voice. When others lose control, maintain yours.

3. *Focus first on areas of agreement.* Always find something to affirm before you counter someone's views.

4. *Weigh criticism objectively.* Listening to gripes is part of leadership.

5. *When you're wrong, admit it.* Those who can't admit error look pathetically insecure. Saying "I was wrong" actually increases your stature.

Bosses squelch conflict. Servant leaders welcome conflict as an opportunity for growth and positive change.

A gentle answer turns away wrath, but a harsh word stirs up anger.
Proverbs 15:1

Maintaining Your Vision in the Valley

Mountaintops inspire leaders, but valleys mature them.
WINSTON CHURCHILL

Os Hillman, president of Marketplace Leaders, gleans fresh insights from a familiar story—the story of a visionary young leader named Joseph.

In Genesis 37, Joseph has what Hillman calls a "mountaintop experience." He enjoys the favor of his father, wears an ornate robe, and dreams of a wonderful future. Joseph had a vision, says Hillman, "a sense of destiny about his life." But before that vision is fulfilled, Joseph must fall from the mountaintop and be tested in the valley.

We all love mountaintop experiences, but character is grown in the valley. "God is a God of the mountain," Hillman says, "but he is even more a God of the valley. In the valley, it is more difficult to see ahead; the clouds often cover the valley and limit our sight."

Betrayed by his brothers, sold into slavery, falsely accused by his employer's wife, and unjustly imprisoned—Joseph was in the depths of the valley. He must have wondered if God had abandoned him. Yet Joseph never let go of the vision God had given him on the mountaintop. He chose to trust God through his valley of adversity.

"God does not waste valley experiences," Hillman concludes. "If we are faithful in the valley, we will enter a new dimension with God that we never thought possible."[147]

Joseph had a dream, and when he told it to his brothers,
they hated him all the more.
GENESIS 37:5

The Talk Show Speech

Leadership is about empathy. It is about having the ability to relate and to connect with people for the purpose of inspiring and empowering their lives.
OPRAH WINFREY

In 1996, when Senator Bob Dole ran against President Bill Clinton, his wife, Elizabeth Dole, gave a convention speech. She told the story of Bob Dole's Kansas childhood, his service in World War II, and his Washington career. She electrified viewers—not only with what she said, but how she said it.

Elizabeth Dole spoke without notes, strolling confidently around the floor. She sometimes paused to touch a woman audience member on the shoulder and talk about how her husband had helped women in the workplace. The audience loved her.

TV cameras caught tears in audience members' eyes as Elizabeth called Bob "the strongest and the most compassionate man I've ever known." She listed her husband's accomplishments with her sunny Carolina charm, and then asked, "I think that's a pretty good record, don't you?" Audience members nodded vigorously.

The media called it "The Talk Show Speech" and compared Elizabeth Dole to Oprah Winfrey. Though Bob Dole was defeated in November, the Talk Show Speech was a big factor in Elizabeth Dole's 2002 election as North Carolina's first woman senator.

The secrets to connecting with your audience: Speak without notes. Move freely and connect through touch. If you're relaxed and confident, your audience will trust you—and follow where you lead.

Gracious words are a honeycomb, sweet to the soul and healing to the bones.
PROVERBS 16:24

The Importance of Small Talk

There are no uninteresting people, only disinterested listeners.
SEAN MCPHEAT

General George S. Patton was known as a driven, often abrasive leader. Yet he loved his soldiers and led from the battlefront, not from a desk. He once said that officers "must be vitally interested in everything that interests the soldier. Usually you will gain a great deal of knowledge by being interested, but even if you do not, the fact that you appear interested has a very high morale influence on the soldier."[148]

Historian Alan Axelrod comments on Patton's advice: "Perhaps the most consistently underrated commodity in business is small talk. Too many managers dismiss it as a waste of time. But 'small talk'—conversation with subordinates that is not exclusively focused on business or on a particular project or task—is vital to creating a bond between [leaders and followers]....

"This does *not* mean faking interest or talking down to employees. It means developing a *genuine* interest in the things that interest them.... Give them what they both want and need: the opportunity for them to identify with you, the person to whom they look for leadership."[149]

As leaders, we want our followers to become enthused about our vision and agenda. If we want them to care about our goals, we need to care about the things that interest them. And that means taking time to *listen*.

Take note of this: Everyone should be quick to listen,
slow to speak, and slow to become angry.
JAMES 1:19

The Unmoving Bar of Character

Leadership is the capacity and will to rally men and women to a common purpose and the character which inspires confidence.
BERNARD "MONTY" MONTGOMERY

Andy Stanley is the senior pastor of Atlanta's North Point Community Church. In *Next Generation Leader*, he writes: "Years ago I adopted a definition of character that is simple enough for me to remember, yet complete enough to have teeth: *Character is the will to do what's right even when it's hard.*

"Character is about *will* because it requires a willingness to make tough decisions—decisions that sometimes run contrary to emotion, intuition, economics, current trends, and in the eyes of some, common sense.... You must decide ahead of time what is nonnegotiable as it relates to right and wrong.

"When we talk about the will to do what's *right*, we are assuming the existence of a standard of right and wrong that exists apart from us, an unmoving bar by which we are measured. Leaders worth following...lead with the assumption that there is a benchmark by which all decisions are judged....

"Character involves doing what's right because it's the right thing to do—regardless of the cost."[150] Do you guard your character regardless of the cost? Or is your character negotiable?

Do not conform to the pattern of this world, but be transformed by the renewing of your mind. Then you will be able to test and approve what God's will is—his good, pleasing, and perfect will.
ROMANS 12:2

Take Charge of Your Leadership Role

*Nothing so conclusively proves a man's ability to lead others
as what he does from day to day to lead himself.*
THOMAS J. WATSON

The late General Norman Schwarzkopf commanded coalition forces in the first Gulf War, 1990–1991. After retiring from the army, Schwarzkopf appeared in a motivational video for business leaders. The video, titled *Taking Charge*, listed seven qualities of a great leader:

1. *Leaders help people succeed.* They aren't threatened by the success of subordinates; they welcome it.

2. *Leaders don't mistake management for leadership.* Managers are concerned with processes and resources. Leaders are concerned with people.

3. *Leaders set goals that anyone can understand.* They state them simply and clearly, avoiding technical jargon.

4. *Leaders set high performance standards.* They know that only the best succeed in a competitive marketplace.

5. *Leaders know there's always room for improvement.* And they continually encourage improvement at every level.

6. *Leaders take charge.* They are responsible, they hold the team accountable, and they execute the plan.

7. *Leaders do what's right.* They lead according to clear ethical principles.[151]

By pursuing these seven qualities, anyone can become a competent leader. By excelling in them, a competent leader can become a great leader.

*Here is a trustworthy saying: Whoever aspires to be
an overseer [leader] desires a noble task.*
1 TIMOTHY 3:1

How to Manage Fear

Courage is being scared to death and saddling up anyway.
JOHN WAYNE

Marshal Ferdinand Foch commanded French forces in World War I. He once learned that a colonel had disciplined a young officer for showing fear in battle. Foch summoned the colonel and reprimanded him harshly, saying, "None but a coward dares to boast that he has never known fear."[152]

We all experience fear, but great leaders learn to manage their fears so that they can continue leading boldly. Here are some suggested ways to manage your fears.

1. *Admit your fears.* There is no shame in being afraid, as long as you don't let fear run your life and stampede your decisions.

2. *Name your fears.* Become clear in your own mind exactly what you are afraid of. Naming your fear is a crucial step toward mastering it.

3. *Recall past experiences with fear.* Think of a time when you were afraid but you continued on in spite of your fear. You've conquered fear in the past, so use that experience to give you confidence going forward.

4. *Decide on a course of action.* Having a clear plan helps dispel fear and keep you moving toward your goals

5. *Meditate on God's Word.* Focus on such passages as Deuteronomy 31:6; Joshua 1; 1 Corinthians 16:13; Ephesians 6:10–18; and 2 Timothy 1:7.

Accept your fear, master it, and continue leading boldly.

> *For God hath not given us the spirit of fear; but of power,*
> *and of love, and of a sound mind.*
> 2 TIMOTHY 1:7 KJV

The Keys to a Serving Heart

The first responsibility of a leader is to define reality.
The last is to say thank you. In between, the leader is a servant.
MAX DE PREE

To have a serving heart, build these six principles into your life:

1. *Servants give up the right to control.* Control freaks need not apply. Herb Kelleher, former CEO of Southwest Airlines, once said, "I've never had any control and I never wanted it. . . . If you're a servant, by definition, you are not controlling."

2. *Serving is an end, not the means to an end.* Serving is not a technique to gain power. A servant serves, expecting nothing in return.

3. *Servants regularly examine and purify their motives.* A. W. Tozer said, "The man who is ambitious to lead is disqualified as a leader."

4. *Servants live a lifestyle of love and caring.* You cannot love people while bossing and intimidating them.

5. *Servants are genuinely humble.* "God sends no one away empty," said Dwight L. Moody, "except those who are full of themselves."

6. *Servants have dirty shoulders.* Gil McGregor taught me the Dirty Shoulders Principle: A servant lets others stand tall on his shoulders—that's why his shoulders are dirty. Servants don't care who gets the glory—they just lift people up.

Be shepherds of God's flock that is under your care, watching over them—
not because you must, but because you are willing, as God wants you to be;
not pursuing dishonest gain, but eager to serve.

1 PETER 5:2

The Next Thought You Think

You must first clearly see a thing in your mind before you can do it.
Alex Morrison

In *Life's Greatest Lessons*, noted writer and speaker Hal Urban tells a pair of stories about the power of a vision to change our world: "In the early 1930s, an engineer named Joseph Strauss went often to a location in San Francisco where he could view the opening of the bay. In his mind he formed a picture of a beautiful bridge connecting the two sides. The more he thought about it, the clearer the picture became."[153]

Under Joseph Strauss's direction, the Golden Gate Bridge was completed in April 1937. Another of his visionary inventions, movable safety netting, saved dozens of lives during construction.

Urban also writes, "When Bill Gates was an undergraduate at Harvard, the personal computer was still in its early stages of development. Most people saw it as a machine to be used for storing large amounts of data.... Gates saw other possibilities. He envisioned then many of the things we do with our computers today.... Pictures in his mind turned into drawings on paper. We know the rest of the story."[154]

Every great invention, every towering structure, every bestselling product began with a vision in the mind of one human being. The next thought you think could change the world.

"You, my son Solomon, acknowledge the God of your father, and serve him with wholehearted devotion and with a willing mind, for the LORD searches every heart and understands every desire and every thought."
1 Chronicles 28:9

When Words Are Deeds

Words can sometimes, in moments of grace, attain the quality of deeds.
ELIE WIESEL

In *Baptism by Fire*, historian Mark K. Updegrove writes about the tremendous power of words in the political realm.

"Words matter. The words spoken by a president at the outset of his term can set the tone of his administration as much as any action he takes. Particularly in a time of crisis, they can quell fear and anxiety, and instill confidence and buoyancy. As former British prime minister Clement Attlee once said,... 'Words at great moments of history are deeds.'... The president's inaugural address is the overture....

The only thing we have to fear is fear itself.
Ask not what your country can do for you—ask what you can do for your country.
Our long national nightmare is over.

"These words are as enduring as nearly any part of the presidential legacy of the man who spoke them. At the time they were offered, they were simply sound bites, memorable rhetoric that struck a chord during a difficult time. They resonated at the moment by extending a promise of sorts, providing a glimpse of the character of the new man in charge. They echoed in history when the promise was fulfilled."[155]

Words matter, and words are deeds. Great leaders shape their times and their legacies by the power of words.

The quiet words of the wise are more to be heeded
than the shouts of a ruler of fools.
ECCLESIASTES 9:17

Great Leaders Develop *More* Leaders

*Everybody at Intuit has two jobs: One is to do their job as it is today.
The other is to figure out how to revolutionize it so they can
do it dramatically better in the future.*

SCOTT COOK

Scott Cook is a former Procter & Gamble executive who founded the software company Intuit in 1983. He is now a billionaire, listed on the Forbes 400. He made the comment above during an interview with *Business 2.0*.

Cook understands what great leaders do. They don't simply stick people in a job and tell them to do as they're told. Great leaders want to develop more leaders. They say, "I believe in you; now believe in yourself. Be a visionary. Be a leader in your own right."[156]

That's what Jesus did with His disciples. According to the Gospel writer Luke, "When Jesus had called the Twelve together, he gave them power and authority to drive out all demons and to cure diseases, and he sent them out to proclaim the kingdom of God and to heal the sick" (Luke 9:1–2).

When you grant "power and authority," your people gain ownership and initiative. They might make some mistakes—the disciples certainly did. But Jesus kept teaching and training, and His followers ultimately started a movement that became worldwide Christianity.

What might your people accomplish with the authority you give them?

*When the crowd saw this, they were filled with awe;
and they praised God, who had given such authority to man.*

MATTHEW 9:8

Are You Grateful—or Do You Feel Cheated?

*No Christian can be a pessimist, for Christianity
is a system of radical optimism.*
WILLIAM RALPH INGE

As historian Stephen Ambrose began work on a three-volume biography of Richard Nixon, he requested an interview with the former president. Mr. Nixon refused the request. Ambrose proceeded to write the biography without Nixon's cooperation.

After the second volume was published, Charlie Rose interviewed Nixon and asked what he thought of the book. "I don't read that stuff," Nixon replied. Rose was incredulous. "Come on," he said. "Of course you read Ambrose." Nixon said, "He's just another left-wing historian."

"I loved the line," Ambrose said later, "because it's so Nixonian." What does Ambrose mean by "Nixonian"? He explained that Nixon was pessimistic and darkly suspicious of the motives of people around him.

"Nixon," he said, "was five times nominated for national office. He won four of those elections. … [Yet he] felt that life cheated him? Isn't that remarkable? … He always questioned the other guy's motives and always figured that they were base."[157]

Great leaders are positive and optimistic. They are grateful for their blessings. They love people and always expect the best of people. What kind of leader are you? Are you a "Nixonian" leader—or a role model of gratitude, optimism, and love for your fellow human beings?

*Finally, brothers and sisters, whatever is true, whatever is noble,
whatever is right, whatever is pure, whatever is lovely, whatever is admirable—
if anything is excellent or praiseworthy—think about such things.*
PHILIPPIANS 4:8

Invest in Your Most Valuable Asset

You can learn anything you need to learn to achieve any goal you set for yourself. . . . There are no limits.
BRIAN TRACY

In *Focal Point*, Brian Tracy underscores the importance of investing in your own competence. "To earn more," he writes, "you must learn more. You must add more value."

Tracy offers a powerful success idea that I myself have adopted and practice every single day: "Invest 3 percent of your income back into yourself for the rest of your life." In other words, invest in your mind, in your knowledge base, in your skill set, in your leadership competence. Over the course of a lifetime, every dollar you invest will be repaid a hundredfold, a thousandfold, or more.

How do you invest in yourself? Buy books in your field of endeavor. Study those books, highlight them, take notes, and build that knowledge into your life. Take classes and attend seminars. Buy audio and video programs. Often just one or two ideas in an entire book or seminar will be worth many times the price you paid.

Brian Tracy tells about a thirty-five-year-old self-employed dad with an eighth-grade education who bought a $60 audio program. This man told Tracy that the information in that program had enabled him to increase his annual income from $30,000 to $304,000. Clearly, that was $60 well-invested.

"You are your most valuable asset," Tracy concludes. "Continually feed your mind to develop more of your potential."[158]

An intelligent heart acquires knowledge,
and the ear of the wise seeks knowledge.
PROVERBS 18:15 ESV

Set Your Face Like Flint

Choose wisely—then act decisively.
JONATHAN LOCKWOOD HUIE

Seven months into President Reagan's first term, thirteen thousand members of PATCO, the Professional Air Traffic Controllers Organization, went on strike, demanding higher pay and shorter hours. Having supported Reagan's candidacy, the union expected Reagan to support their cause, though the strike violated federal law. But Reagan ordered controllers to return to work in forty-eight hours or be fired. The strike continued—so Reagan fired them all.

After that, anyone negotiating with Ronald Reagan (including the Soviets), knew he meant what he said. In *Reagan on Leadership*, James M. Strock suggests several leadership lessons we can learn from this incident.

"Recognize that a willingness to take decisive action is a hallmark of an effective leader—people want to know where you stand so they will know where they stand.

"Decisive action must be taken in a timely manner—an action taken too late, even if executed with greater precision, may have much less value.

"Decisive actions that put the leader at visible risk set an example that strengthens the organization.

"By aligning words and deeds, decisive actions add predictability and certainty to an enterprise.

"A leader should make plain, both before and after decisive actions are taken, how their accomplishment relates to the vision of the organization."[159]

To be respected as a strong leader, decide firmly and always keep your word.

*Because the Sovereign LORD helps me, I will not be disgraced. Therefore
have I set my face like flint, and I know I will not be put to shame.*
ISAIAH 50:7

The Next Generation of Servant Leaders

*A servant leader is thinking about the next generation,
the next leader, the next opportunity.*
Skip Pritchard

D r. L. Paige Patterson, president of Southwestern Baptist Theological Seminary, told me that he first learned about servant leadership as a teenager. "My parents raised me to be a leader," he said. "My mother told me I was an answer to prayer and that God had something strategically important for me to do in life. My father told me to seek the highest level of service to Jesus and others.

"When I was sixteen, my father took me around the world. I had the privilege of preaching in churches in many countries, including Korea. This was shortly after the Korean War. My parents were instrumental in facilitating the adoption of many Korean orphans by people in America.

"One evening, I preached at a church in Baytown, Texas, and made an appeal on behalf of Korean orphans. An oil company engineer asked me about the adoption process. They eventually adopted a little boy. I was surprised to learn that they named him after me.

"It was a profound experience for a sixteen-year-old to be used by God to impact lives around the world. I'd like to see thousands of young people experience the lasting joy of service to others. Leadership begins with serving."

Great leaders continually seek to raise up the *next* generation of servant leaders.

*[John the Baptist, speaking of Jesus]:
"He must become greater; I must become less."*
John 3:30

A Vision Unchained

I dream of the realization of the unity of Africa, whereby its leaders combine in their efforts to solve the problems of this continent.
NELSON MANDELA

Carmine Gallo is an author, speaker, and leadership expert. In *Ten Simple Secrets of the World's Greatest Business Communicators*, he writes: "Few visions have had as profound an impact as Nelson Mandela's 'dream of an Africa which is in peace with itself.' Mandela spent more than twenty-seven years in prison for fighting to improve the plight of black South Africa during a time of white minority rule. Mandela was set free after South Africa abolished apartheid. He was awarded the Nobel Peace Prize and served as the first black South African president....

"The years he spent in a notorious Cape Town prison only strengthened his resolve to change the way his countrymen lived together. His vision saw him through those years and inspired hundreds of millions of people. . . . He knew where he wanted to lead his people and how to get there.... Where do you want to take your company? How will you get there? Above all, have you communicated this vision to the people who serve with you?"[160]

A vision of a brighter future, communicated with passion and conviction, is a powerful means of inspiring and motivating your team, your organization, your church—or even your nation.

Because of my chains, most of the brothers and sisters have become confident in the Lord and dare all the more to proclaim the gospel without fear.
PHILIPPIANS 1:14

Be Unforgettable When You Speak

*This is fantastic! I never made it to college—I didn't have enough money—
and I decided I was going to be a writer anyway.*
RAY BRADBURY, TO THE CALTECH CLASS OF 2000

D o you recall your college commencement address? Probably not. But here are some excerpts from commencement speeches that surely made a lasting impression.

Rock star Bono, to the University of Pennsylvania class of 2004: "America is not just a country, it's an idea. . . . The idea that anything is possible, that's one of the reasons why I'm a fan of America. It's like, hey, look there's the moon up there, let's take a walk on it, bring back a piece of it. That's the kind of America that I'm a fan of."[161]

Apple cofounder Steve Jobs, one year after his cancer diagnosis, to Stanford's class of 2005: "Your time is limited, so don't waste it living someone else's life. Don't be trapped by dogma, which is living with the results of other people's thinking. Don't let the noise of others' opinions drown out your own inner voice, heart, and intuition."[162]

TV producer Aaron Sorkin, to Syracuse University's class of 2012: "Make no mistake about it, you are dumb. You're a group of incredibly well-educated dumb people. I was there. We all were there. You're barely functional."[163]

Great speeches are memorable. They disturb our thinking and grip our emotions. Great leaders give memorable speeches that affect us at a deep level.

*The wise in heart are called discerning,
and gracious words promote instruction.*
PROVERBS 16:21

Motivated by Love

Love is the force that ignites the spirit and binds teams together.
Phil Jackson

Coaching," writes ESPN's Bill Simmons, "isn't just about calling plays. . . . It's management more than anything else. You manage people." Former NBA coach Phil Jackson "managed people better than anyone."

Phil Jackson was a special coach, Simmons explains, because "he cared about his twelfth guy as much as his best guy. He spent time with his players, bought them gifts, thought about what made them tick. He connected with them, sold them on the concept of a team, stuck up for them when they needed him. . . . His players competed for him for many reasons, but mainly because they truly believed Jackson cared about them. Which he definitely did."[164]

In his book *Sacred Hoops*, Jackson recalls that Bulls co-owner Jerry Reinsdorf claimed that most people are motivated by either fear or greed. Jackson writes, "I countered that they are motivated by their community and by love." His Bulls and Lakers teams, he added, clearly played for love for one another and love for the game. "As a result of our connectedness and mindfulness," Jackson concludes, "we produced some wonderful results."[165]

How do you lead your team, your organization, or your church? Do you motivate through fear or greed—or love? Are you just calling plays—or are you managing a close-knit community of people?

As each has received a gift, use it to serve one another,
as good stewards of God's varied grace.
1 Peter 4:10 esv

"To Be Credible, We Must Be Truthful"

It's not enough to rage against the lie.
You've got to replace it with the truth.
BONO

During World War II, CBS newsman Edward R. Murrow stood on London rooftops, broadcasting news of the Blitz while Hitler's bombs rained down. Murrow also rode along on more than twenty Allied bombing raids over Germany and was one of the first Americans to report from the death camps of the Holocaust.

Murrow's distinctive voice was well known to radio listeners. After the war, millions more came to recognize his trademark Camel cigarette. A three-pack-a-day smoker, Murrow was the first to report (in his *See It Now* TV series) on the link between smoking and cancer. He truthfully told viewers, "I doubt I could spend a half hour without a cigarette."

Edward R. Murrow's investigative reports eventually led to a showdown in the office of CBS chairman William S. Paley, who told Murrow he was tired of the "stomachaches" the news program caused. Murrow severed his ties with CBS in 1961, accepting an appointment from President Kennedy to head the United States Information Agency.[166] He died in 1965 at age fifty-seven.

Murrow once summed up his views on honesty and integrity as the foundation of good journalism: "To be persuasive, we must be believable; to be believable, we must be credible; to be credible, we must be truthful."

"These are the things you are to do: Speak the truth to each other,
and render true and sound judgment in your courts."
ZECHARIAH 8:16

A Commentary on Jack's Rules

An organization's ability to learn, and translate that learning into action rapidly, is the ultimate competitive advantage.

JACK WELCH

While Jack Welch was CEO of General Electric (1981–2001), GE's value rose 4,000 percent. The wisdom he accumulated is summed up as Jack Welch's Six Rules.[167] Here's my biblical commentary on those rules:

Rule 1: Control your own destiny or someone else will. Jeremiah 29:11 says God has "plans to prosper you." To control your own destiny, entrust yourself to Him.

Rule 2: Face reality as it is, not as it was or as you wish it were. Those without faith in God think spiritual reality is "foolishness" (1 Corinthians 2:14). To face reality, follow the teachings of Jesus—and "the truth will set you free" (John 8:32).

Rule 3: Be candid with everyone. "Do not lie" (Colossians 3:9). Transparent honesty is a biblical requirement—and it's good for business.

Rule 4: Don't manage, lead. Leaders take their followers "along unfamiliar paths" (Isaiah 42:16), and "lead them out and bring them in" (Numbers 27:17).

Rule 5: Change before you have to. God says, "New things I declare; before they spring into being I announce them to you" (Isaiah 42:9). Leaders are nimble and flexible, eagerly embracing change.

Rule 6: If you don't have a competitive advantage, don't compete. Our competitive advantage is God. He calls us to "run in such a way as to get the prize" (1 Corinthians 9:24).

Where there is no guidance, a people falls,
but in an abundance of counselors there is safety.

PROVERBS 11:14 ESV

An Example of Bold Perseverance

I wish to have no connection with any ship that does not sail fast;
for I intend to go in harm's way
JOHN PAUL JONES

On September 23, 1779, American naval officer John Paul Jones commanded the warship *Le Bonhomme Richard* off the northeast coast of England. There he encountered a British merchant convoy escorted by the royal warship *Serapis*. The British ship attacked the *Richard*, pounding the American ship with forty-four guns roaring.

Though the *Richard's* hull was riddled with holes, Jones sent his ship straight into the enemy fire, colliding with *Serapis*. He ordered his men to lash the *Richard's* bowsprit to the British ship's mizzenmast. As both ships continued blazing away at point-blank range, the British commander, Richard Pearson, demanded Jones's surrender.

Jones later recalled, "I answered him in the most determined negative." His exact words are unknown, but these defiant words are attributed to him: "I have not yet begun to fight!"

Minutes later, one of the American shots found its mark, touching off an explosion aboard the *Serapis*. As a result, Commander Pearson surrendered to John Paul Jones. Though *Le Bonhomme Richard* sank minutes later, Jones and his crew seized *Serapis* as their prize. The story of John Paul Jones entered history as a great example of the mighty power of perseverance and bold leadership.

Blessed is the one who perseveres under trial because, having stood the test,
that person will receive the crown of life that the Lord
has promised to those who love him.

JAMES 1:12

The Extra Mile Principle

*Thousands of books have been written on leadership, but few on servanthood.
Everyone wants to lead; no one wants to be a servant.*
RICK WARREN

In the Sermon on the Mount, Jesus said, "If anyone forces you to go one mile, go with them two miles" (Matthew 5:41). He referred to a Roman practice called "impressment." Soldiers of Rome could force civilians to carry their burdens without compensation.

Jesus was saying, "If a soldier orders you to go one mile with him, voluntarily go two. Show him your serving heart. Without complaining, do twice as much as your enemy demands of you." I call this the Extra Mile Principle.

Imagine how your business, team, church, or military unit would be altered if you and your people practiced the Extra Mile Principle. How might it affect relationships and conflicts? How might it impact morale and motivation?

The extra mile means doing more than is required. It means confronting evil with good. It means responding to mistreatment with unconditional love and forgiveness.

Remember, Jesus went the extra mile for you and me. When Roman soldiers forced Him to carry a cross He didn't deserve, He went the extra mile. What unfair burden are you willing to carry to follow in His footsteps?

*In your relationships with one another, have the same mindset as
Christ Jesus. . . . He made himself nothing by taking the very
nature of a servant. . . . He humbled himself by becoming
obedient to death—even death on a cross!*
PHILIPPIANS 2:5, 7–8

A Legacy of Leadership

Leadership is action, not position.
DONALD H. MCGANNON

At the end of my senior year at Wake Forest, our baseball team played in the NCAA regional tournament in Gastonia, North Carolina. My family came from Wilmington, Delaware—my mom and sisters in one car and my dad in another.

After we lost the twelve-inning final game to Florida State, I was moody when I thanked my family for coming. I wish I'd been more gracious. When I got home a few days later, Mom told me that Dad had been killed in a single-car accident while driving home from the game.

The newspaper honored him with an editorial. Here's an excerpt: "A ready smile, a steady eye, a bone-crushing handshake—these were some of the attributes of James W. Williams, whose life was cut short at fifty-three in an automobile accident Tuesday night. It's difficult to accept his death, for Jim Williams was rock-like in his integrity and steadfast in his duties as a citizen.

"His labors on behalf of Delaware's retarded children go back many years.

"Jim Williams was an active, loyal Democrat, but when his keen sense of right and wrong was offended, he exposed wrongdoing regardless of the cost. Delaware has lost one of its very finest citizens just when it needs him most."

When *your* life is over, what will your leadership legacy be?

*"Whoever heard me spoke well of me, and those who saw me
commended me, because I rescued the poor who cried for help,
and the fatherless who had none to assist them."*

JOB 29:11–12

Our Ultimate Leadership Role Model

The greatest leader is not necessarily the one who does the greatest things. He is the one that gets the people to do the greatest things.
Ronald Reagan

Leadership is working through people to achieve a vision or goal. Jesus envisioned "the kingdom of heaven," and His goal was establishing His church.

To fulfill that vision and achieve that goal, He chose twelve men of untested ability. Had I conducted the job interviews, these men wouldn't have made the first cut. But Jesus saw potential that most of us would miss—and He poured His life into them.

Jesus pioneered a leadership model that is now the benchmark for how leadership should be done. It consisted of three key components.

1. *Mentoring*. Jesus invested in the Twelve through relationships. He spent time with them as individuals, building traits of faith, courage, humility, and integrity.

2. *Coaching*. Jesus coached the Twelve to build skills and confidence. He stimulated thinking with parables and open-ended questions. He put them in challenging situations, applauded successes, corrected failures, and cheered them on.

3. *Delegating*. In His early ministry, Jesus preached and healed while the disciples watched. Later, Jesus watched while the disciples preached and healed. He weaned them from dependence on Him and gave them authority to act in His name.

With this leadership model, Jesus molded the Twelve into an unstoppable force for spiritual and social transformation. Who are you training for leadership today?

Jesus called his twelve disciples to him and gave them authority to drive out impure spirits and to heal every disease and sickness.
Matthew 10:1

Notes

1 Bobby Bowden, *Called to Coach: Reflections on Life, Faith and Football* (New York: Simon & Schuster, 2011), 55.

2 John C. Maxwell, *Be All You Can Be* (Colorado Springs: David C. Cook, 2007), 51–52.

3 Ross Bernstein, *World Series Winners: What It Takes to Claim Baseball's Ultimate Prize* (Chicago: Triumph Books, 2012), 111.

4 Ibid., 131.

5 Dave Kraft, *Leaders Who Last* (Wheaton, IL: Crossway, 2010), 99–100.

6 Scott S. Smith, "Gen. Matthew Ridgway Turned The Korean War's Tide," *Investor's Business Daily*, December 4, 2012; http://news.investors.com/management-leaders-in-success/120412-635614-matthew-ridgway-turned-the-tide-in-the-korean-war.htm?p=full.

7 Ibid.

8 Bill Byrd, *Sweet Success: Twelve Proven Habits of Winning Leaders* (Grand Rapids: Revell, 2004), 54.

9 Adam Bryant, "Leadership Never Looks Prepackaged," *New York Times*, August 18, 2012; http://www.nytimes.com/2012/08/19/business/james-hackett-of-steelcase-on-authentic-leadership.html?_r=0.

10 Joy Covey, "A Conversation with Joy Covey," *Harvard Law Bulletin*, summer 2002; http://www.law.harvard.edu/news/bulletin/2002/summer/closing_main.html.

11 Joy Covey, "Return to the Wild: Releasing a Mexican Gray Wolf in the Forests of Arizona," *OnEarth*, June 13, 2011; http://www.onearth.org/blog/mexican-gray-wolf.

12 A. W. Tozer, *The Price of Neglect* (Camp Hill, PA: Christian Publications, 1991), 141.

13 Jon Miller, *Confessions of a Baseball Purist* (New York: Simon & Schuster, 1998), 165–166.

14 Robert Safian, "This is Generation Flux: Meet the Pioneers of the New (and Chaotic) Frontier of Business," *Fast Company*, January 9, 2012; http://www.fastcompany.com/1802732/generation-flux-meet-pioneers-new-and-chaotic-frontier-business.

[15] John J. Pitney, Jr., *The Art of Political Warfare* (Norman, OK: University of Oklahoma Press, 2000), 58.

[16] Terry Eastland, "Mr. Compassionate Conservative," *The Weekly Standard*, August 7, 2006; http://www.weeklystandard.com/Content/Public/Articles/000/000/012/511umjoo.asp.

[17] Christine Brennan, "Sports Left Dimmed by Their Dark Side in 2012," *USA Today*, December 27, 2012, Sports 3C.

[18] Ibid.

[19] BBC, "Lance Armstrong: USADA Report Labels Him 'A Serial Cheat,'" BBC.co.uk, October 11, 2012; http://www.bbc.co.uk/sport/0/cycling/19903716.

[20] *Investor's Business Daily*, "IBD's Ten Secrets to Success," Purdue University, College of Consumer and Family Sciences, May 8, 2005; http://www.cfs.purdue.edu/CSR/courses/csr309/documents/IBDs10SecretstoSuccess.pdf.

[21] Associated Press, "Winfrey Says She Wants to Nurture Kids," *Washington Post*, January 3, 2007; http://www.washingtonpost.com/wp-dyn/content/article/2007/01/03/AR2007010301020.html.

[22] Patricia Edmonds, "This Time, I Won't Fail," *USA Weekend*, December 17, 2006; http://159.54.226.237/06_issues/061217/061217oprah.html.

[23] Lawrence A. Pervin, *Football's New York Giants: A History* (Jefferson, NC: McFarland, 2009), 113.

[24] John Maxymuk, "Giants Stadium Countdown: Tiki Honors Mara," *New York Times*, November 17, 2009; http://fifthdown.blogs.nytimes.com/2009/11/17/giants-stadium-countdown-tiki-honors-mara/?scp=3&sq=Wellington+Mara+Redskins+died&st=nyt.

[25] Biz Plus Poll, "Chief Example Officer?" *San Francisco Business Times*, May 27, 2007; http://www.bizjournals.com/eastbay/stories/2007/05/28/editorial1.html?page=all.

[26] "To Lead, Promote Yourself to 'CEO,'" ManageBetter.biz, December 23, 2012, adapted from the Management Centre Europe website; http://www.managementresources.com/Main/Articles/To_lead_promote_yourself_to_CEO__22528.aspx.

[27] Adelia Cellini Linecker, "Early Lesson: Flexibility Leads to Creativity at Work," *Investor's Business Daily*, January 9, 2013; http://news.investors.com/management-leaders-in-success/010913-639886-self-directed-learning-freedom-creativity-entrepreneur-montessori.htm.

[28] Nancy Luna, "Attack of the Double-Double," *D* magazine, March 2011; http://www.dmagazine.com/Home/D_Magazine/2011/March/How_In_N_Out_Burger_Will_Change_Dallas_Fast_Food_02.aspx?p=1; Russ Parsons, "A Day in the Life, at 90," *Los Angeles Times*, August 7, 2002; http://articles.latimes.com/2002/aug/07/food/fo-julia7.

[29] "In-N-Out Burger History," In-N-Out Burger Company Store; http://shop.in-n-out.com/history.aspx.

[30] Ellen Florian, "Robert Shiller: The Best Advice I Ever Got," CNN.com, December 2, 2011; http://money.cnn.com/2011/12/01/news/economy/robert_shiller_best_advice.fortune/index.htm.

[31] Jack Ramsay, "My Secrets to NBA Head Coaching Success," ESPN.com: NBA, September 19, 2002; http://sports.espn.go.com/nba/columns/story?columnist=ramsay_drjack&id=1434127.

[32] Ibid.

[33] Ibid.

[34] Michael Useem, "America's Best Leaders: Indra Nooyi, PepsiCo CEO," *U.S. News & World Report*, November 19, 2008; http://www.usnews.com/news/best-leaders/articles/2008/11/19/americas-best-leaders-indra-nooyi-pepsico-ceo?page=2.

[35] "Previous Daily Quotes Page 7," LadyMustangs.com; http://www.ladymustangs.com/dailyquotespage7.htm.

[36] Bertrand Russell, *Education and the Social Order* (London: Routledge, 2002), 73.

[37] David Timms, *The Power of Blessing: How a Carefully Chosen Word Changes Everything* (Minneapolis: Bethany House, 2010), 89-90.

[38] Flavio Martins, "Richard Branson's Seven Customer Service Success Rules To Live By," CustomerThink.com, April 2, 2012; http://www.customerthink.com/blog/7_customer_service_rules_from_richard_branson_ceo_of_virgin.

[39] Nancy F. Koehn, "Lincoln's School of Management," *New York Times*, January 26, 2013; http://www.nytimes.com/2013/01/27/business/abraham-lincoln-as-management-guru.html?pagewanted=all&_r=0.

[40] George Manning and Kent Curtis, *The Art of Leadership* (New York: McGraw-Hill Higher Education, 2003), 340.

[41] Koehn, "Lincoln's School of Management."

[42] Michael Mink, "Dean Smith, The King of Carolina Basketball," *Investor's Business Daily*, January 23, 2013; http://news.investors.com/management-leaders-in-success/012313-641603-coach-dean-smith-winning-carolina-basketball-olympics.htm?p=full.

[43] John W. Drakeford, *The Awesome Power of Positive Attention* (Nashville: Broadman, 1991), 73–74

[44] Horace Porter, *Campaigning with Grant* (New York: Century Co., 1907), 316.

[45] Bill Dann, "Leadership Is Not a Democracy," Professional Growth Systems, November 2, 2012; http://www.professionalgrowthsystems.com/its-not-a-democracy.html.

[46] Don Soderquist, *Live, Learn, Lead to Make a Difference* (Nashville: J Countryman, 2006), 29–31.

[47] Michael Mink, "Martin Luther King Jr. Learned from His Father and Led," *Investor's Business Daily*, January 18, 2013; http://news.investors.com/management-leaders-in-success/011813-641215-martin-luther-king-jr-sr-daddy-rev.htm?p=full.

[48] Bonnie Angelo, *First Mothers* (New York: HarperCollins, 2009), 302–303.

[49] Lou Cannon, *President Reagan: The Role of a Lifetime* (New York: Public Affairs, 2000), 20.

[50] Al Browning, *I Remember Paul Bear Bryant* (Nashville: Cumberland House, 2001), xxii.

[51] Drew Roberts, "Top Fifty Quotes from Bear Bryant," Saturday Down South, August 7, 2012; http://www.saturdaydownsouth.com/2012/bear-bryant-50-quotes/.

52 Sandy Smith, "NSC 2012: Captain Sully Sullenberger Talks About the Miracle on the Hudson River," Environment Health Safety Today, EHSToday.com, October 22, 2012; http://ehstoday.com/safety/nsc-2012-captain-sully-sullenberger-talks-about-miracle-hudson-river.

53 Jane E. Allen, "Congressmen Permitted to Enter Soviet Prison Camp," Associated Press, AP News Archive, August 8, 1989; http://www.apnewsarchive.com/1989/Congressmen-Permitted-to-Enter-Soviet-Prison-Camp/id-73f31ca37471b6873a0c4ffb74285553.

54 Charles Colson, "Putting Our Faith on the Line," *Decision* magazine, October 1, 2012; http://www.billygraham.org/articlepage.asp?articleid=8953.

55 Dong-Phuong Nguyen, "Tony Dungy Surprises Students at Pride Elementary," *Tampa Bay Times*, November 16, 2012; http://www.tampabay.com/news/humaninterest/tony-dungy-surprises-students-at-pride-elementary/1261780.

56 Associated Press, "Quotes on Retirement of Tony Dungy," *USA Today*, January 12, 2009; http://usatoday30.usatoday.com/sports/football/nfl/2009-01-12-1693403345_x.htm.

57 Colson, "Putting Our Faith on the Line."

58 Colin Powell, "The Best of Our Advice," CNN.com, October 25, 2012; http://money.cnn.com/gallery/news/companies/2012/10/25/best-of-best-advice.fortune/16.html.

59 Jessen O'Brien, "Bend, Not Break: Leadership Lessons for Resilience amid Struggle," *Fast Company*, January 3, 2013; http://www.fastcompany.com/3004166/bend-not-break-leadership-lessons-resilience-amid-struggle.

60 "Chick-fil-A's Closed-On-Sunday Policy," TruettCathy.com; http://www.truettcathy.com/pdfs/ClosedonSunday.pdf.

61 Jim Brown, "Pastor's Pen," March 28, 2012, Monterey Baptist Church, March 28, 2012; http://montereybaptist.org/wp/?p=595.

62 James Carville and Paul Begala, *Buck Up, Suck Up...and Come Back When You Foul Up* (New York: Simon & Schuster, 2003), 36–37.

[63] Elise Labott, "Clinton: I'm Responsible for Diplomats' Security," CNN, October 16, 2012; http://www.cnn.com/2012/10/15/us/clinton-benghazi/index.html.

[64] John M. Broder, "Familiar Fallback for Officials: 'Mistakes Were Made,'" *New York Times*, March 14, 2007; http://www.nytimes.com/2007/03/14/washington/14mistakes.html?_r=2&oref=slogin&.

[65] Ronald Reagan, Address before a Joint Session of Congress on the State of the Union, January 27, 1987, The American Presidency Project; http://www.presidency.ucsb.edu/ws/index.php?pid=34430.

[66] NPR and wire reports, "Obama, Bank Leaders Discuss 'Toxic Assets,'" NPR.org, March 27, 2009; http://www.npr.org/templates/story/story.php?storyId=102447466.

[67] Emily Holbrook, "Do Quiet Leaders Make Better Leaders?" Risk Management Monitor, June 26, 2012; http://www.riskmanagementmonitor.com/do-quiet-leaders-make-better-leaders/.

[68] Karl Moore, "Introverts No Longer the Quiet Followers of Extroverts," *Forbes*, August 22, 2012; http://www.forbes.com/sites/karlmoore/2012/08/22/introverts-no-longer-the-quiet-followers-of-extroverts/.

[69] Robert W. Merry, *Where They Stand: The American Presidents in the Eyes of Voters and Historians* (New York: Simon & Schuster, 2012), Kindle edition, np.

[70] Daniel Harkavy, *Becoming a Coaching Leader* (Nashville: Thomas Nelson, 2007), 79.

[71] Adam Bryant, *The Corner Office* (New York: Times Books, 2011), 91–92.

[72] Jack Welch with John A. Byrne, *Jack: Straight from the Gut* (New York: Warner, 2003), 27–29.

[73] Jeff Janssen, *Championship Team Building* (Tucson, AZ: Winning the Mental Game, 1999), 58.

[74] Marty Schottenheimer, "Creating a Winning Environment," in Ray Didinger, *Game Plans for Success* (New York: McGraw-Hill Professional, 1996), 17–18.

[75] Robert Ajemian, "Where Is the Real George Bush?" *Time*, January 26, 1987; http://www.time.com/time/magazine/article/0,9171,963342-2,00.html.

[76] Martin J. Medhurst, *The Rhetorical Presidency of George H. W. Bush* (College Station: Texas A&M University Press, 2006), 34.

[77] Julian Robertson, "The Best of Our Advice," CNN.com, October 25, 2012; http://money.cnn.com/gallery/news/companies/2012/10/25/best-of-best-advice.fortune/18.html.

[78] Ron Willingham, *The People Principle* (New York: Macmillan, 1999), 125.

[79] Ibid.

[80] Philip Yancey, *Grace Notes* (Grand Rapids: Zondervan, 2009), 263.

[81] Antonia Felix, *Condi: The Condoleezza Rice Story* (New York: Newmarket Press, 2005), 121.

[82] Ibid., 116.

[83] Ibid., 117.

[84] Ibid., 118.

[85] Harvard Business Review, *HBR's Ten Must Reads on Managing People* (Boston: Harvard Business Press, 2011), 12–13.

[86] Gregg Rosenthal, "Steve Sabol, President of NFL Films, Dies," NFL.com, September 18, 2012; http://www.nfl.com/news/story/0ap1000000063643/article/steve-sabol-president-of-nfl-films-dies.

[87] Joe Klein, *The Natural: The Misunderstood Presidency of Bill Clinton* (New York: Random House, 2002), 195–196.

[88] Terry Felber, *Am I Making Myself Clear? Secrets of the World's Greatest Communicators* (Nashville: Thomas Nelson, 2002), 108–111.

[89] Jack Uldrich, *Soldier, Statesman, Peacemaker* (New York: AMACOM, 2005), 95–96.

[90] David Foster, *A Renegade's Guide to God* (New York: FaithWords, 2006), 223.

[91] Brian Tracy, *TurboStrategy* (New York: AMACOM, 2003), 50.

[92] John Baldoni, "Ask Three Questions to Clarify Expectations," *Harvard Business Review*, HBR Blog Network, August 18, 2009; http://blogs.hbr.org/baldoni/2009/08/three_questions_to_clarify.html.

[93] Ben Horowitz, "In Defense of Standards, Ethics, and Honest Financial Reporting at Hewlett-Packard," *Fast Company*, October 10, 2010; http://

www.fastcompany.com/1694243/defense-standards-ethics-and-honest-financial-reporting-hewlett-packard.

94 Lawrence Block, "Great Moments in Contemporary Publishing," LB's Blog, February 14, 2013; http://lawrenceblock.wordpress.com/2013/02/14/great-moments-in-contemporary-publishing/.

95 David Baron, *Moses on Management* (New York: Pocket Books, 1999), 230–232.

96 Chuck Colson, "At the Foot of the Cross," BreakPoint.org, January 6, 2004; https://www.breakpoint.org/bpcommentaries/entry/13/12302.

97 Brian Billick, *Competitive Leadership* (Chicago: Triumph Books, 2001), 72.

98 Michael R. Beschloss, *Presidential Courage* (New York: Simon & Schuster, 2008), 269–271.

99 John Maxwell, *The Maxwell Leadership Bible, NKJV* (Nashville: Thomas Nelson, 2003), Kindle edition, np.

100 Shawn Parr, "Disruptive Innovation, Dog-Food Edition," *Fast Company*, January 13, 2012; http://www.fastcompany.com/1808050/disruptive-innovation-dog-food-edition.

101 David Shula, "Don Shula's Enshrinement Speech Transcript," Pro Football Hall of Fame, Canton, Ohio, July 26, 1997; http://www.profootballhof.com/history/release.aspx?release_id=2101.

102 Ron Willingham, *The People Principle* (New York: St. Martin's, 1999), 42–43.

103 Bill Pennington, *The Heisman* (New York: HarperCollins, 2004), 162–163.

104 Mark Eppler, *The Wright Way* (New York: AMACOM, 2004), 89, 173.

105 Terry Newell, "Wanted: Leaders Who Tell the Truth?" The Blog, *Huffington Post*, May 31, 2010; http://www.huffingtonpost.com/terry-newell/wanted-leaders-who-tell-t_b_595147.html.

106 Cheryl Dahle, "Natural Leader: Confidence and Competence," *Fast Company*, November 30, 2000; http://www.fastcompany.com/41118/natural-leader-continued.

107 Terry Brighton, *Patton, Montgomery, Rommel: Masters of War* (New York: Crown, 2008), 135.

[108] Lucy McCauley, "Next Stop—The 21st Century," *Fast Company*, August 31, 1999; http://www.fastcompany.com/37421/next-stop-21st-century.

[109] Rick Warren, "What's the Difference between Managing and Leading?" *Christian Post*, October 17, 2005; http://www.christianpost.com/news/what-s-the-difference-between-managing-and-leading-13770/.

[110] Ernie Harwell, "Flashback: Ernie Harwell on Sparky Anderson," *Detroit Free Press*, November 4, 2010; http://www.freep.com/article/20101104/SPORTS02/101104083/Flashback-Ernie-Harwell-Sparky-Anderson.

[111] Sam Smith, "Inside the NBA: Bummer of a Trade in 2000 Haunts Bulls, *Chicago Tribune*, October 20, 2003; http://articles.chicagotribune.com/2003-10-20/sports/0310200246_1_bulls-steve-francis-fair-warning.

[112] John Coleman, "To Find a Way Forward, Leaders Must Embrace the Lost Art of Compromise," *Fast Company*, November 20, 2012; http://www.fastcompany.com/3003284/find-way-forward-leaders-must-embrace-lost-art-compromise.

[113] Charles Francis, *Wisdom Well Said* (El Prado, NM: Levine Mesa Press, 2009), 60.

[114] Thomas J. Watson, Jr., *Father, Son & Co.* (New York: Bantam, 1991), 316.

[115] Russ Mitchell, "Medical Wonder: Meet the CEO Who Rebuilt a Crumbling California Hospital," *Fast Company*, May 2, 2011; http://www.fastcompany.com/1747629/medical-wonder-meet-ceo-who-rebuilt-crumbling-california-hospital.

[116] John MacArthur, *Hard to Believe* (Nashville: Thomas Nelson, 2003), 58–59.

[117] Bob Oates, *Football in America: Game of the Century* (Coal Valley, IL: Quality Sports Publications, 1999), 232.

[118] Bob Starkey, "The Other Side of Vince Lombardi," Hoops Thoughts, October 2, 2009; http://hoopthoughts.blogspot.com/2009/10/other-side-of-vince-lombardi.html.

[119] Chris Havel, *Lombardi: An Illustrated Life* (Iola, WI: Krause Publications, 2011), 62.

[120] Jim Denney, "Darwin's Holocaust?" The Truth Will Make You Mad, June 20, 2012; http://thetruthwillmakeyoumad.wordpress.com/2012/06/20/darwins-holocaust-part-1-of-3/.

[121] William R. Coulson, Ph.D., "Founder of 'Values-Free' Education 'Owes Parents an Apology,'" *AFA Journal*, April 1989; http://www.newyorkeagleforum.org/esteem/esteem_articles/coulson.html.

[122] Manny Fernandez and Michael Schwirtz, "Untouchable in Iraq, Ex-Sniper Dies in a Shooting Back Home," *New York Times*, February 3, 2013; http://www.nytimes.com/2013/02/04/us/chris-kyle-american-sniper-author-reported-killed.html.

[123] David Olive, *The Quotable Tycoon* (Naperville, IL: Sourcebooks, 2004), 149.

[124] Bob Briner, *Leadership Lessons of Jesus* (Nashville: B&H, 2008), 26–27.

[125] Smithsonian, "A Fork in the River," *Smithsonian* magazine, June 2005; http://www.smithsonianmag.com/history-archaeology/fork-in-the-river.html.

[126] Donald T. Phillips, *Martin Luther King, Jr., on Leadership* (New York: Warner, 1998), 307.

[127] Hermann Hesse, *The Journey to the East* (New York: Picador, 1956), 38.

[128] Robert K. Greenleaf, *Servant Leadership* (Mahwah, NJ: Paulist Press, 2002), 21; italics in the original.

[129] James M. Kouzes and Barry Z. Posner, *A Leader's Legacy* (San Francisco: Jossey-Bass, 2006), 107.

[130] Ibid., 108; italics in the original.

[131] Dale Carnegie, *How to Win Friends and Influence People* (New York: Simon & Schuster, 1998) 76–77.

[132] Kerry Larkan, *The Talent War: How to Find and Retain the Best People for Your Company* (Tarrytown, NY: Marshall Cavendish, 2006), 171.

[133] Mark Robert Polelle, *Leadership: Fifty Great Leaders and the Worlds They Made* (Westport, CT: Greenwood, 2008), xiv.

[134] Henry T. Blackaby and Richard Blackaby, *Spiritual Leadership: Moving People to God's Agenda* (Nashville: B&H, 2001), 113.

[135] John W. Collis, *The Seven Fatal Management Sins* (Boca Raton: CRC Press, 1998), 125.

[136] Harvey Mackay, "Be a Servant Leader, Not a Self-Serving Leader," *The Arizona Republic*, September 30, 2012; http://www.azcentral.com/arizonarepublic/business/articles/20120927servant-leader-not-self-serving-leader.html.

[137] Ken Blanchard, *The Heart of a Leader* (Colorado Springs: David C. Cook, 2007), 159.

[138] Jack Welch, "Jack Welch's Lessons for Success," CNNMoney, January 25, 1993; http://money.cnn.com/magazines/fortune/fortune_archive/1993/01/25/77396/index.htm.

[139] Bill Catlette and Richard Hadden, *Contented Cows Still Give Buttermilk*, revised edition (Hoboken, NJ: Wiley, 2012), 57.

[140] Robert Mondavi, *Harvests of Joy* (New York: Harcourt, 1998), 143.

[141] Warren G. Bennis and Burt Nanus, *Leaders: Strategies for Taking Charge* (New York: HarperCollins, 2012), 61.

[142] Thomas Huynh, "Interview with Charles Krulak," Sonshi.com; http://www.sonshi.com/krulak.html.

[143] Ken Rosenthal, *Dean Smith: A Tribute* (Champaign, IL: Sports Publishing, 2001), 95–96.

[144] William Taylor, "Do You Pass the Leadership Test?" *Fast Company*, August 4, 2010; http://www.fastcompany.com/1678064/do-you-pass-leadership-test.

[145] "Land the Shuttle," *Chicago Tribune*, August 28, 2010; http://articles.chicagotribune.com/2010-08-28/news/ct-edit-shuttle-20100828_1_space-truck-shuttle-hubble-space-telescope.

[146] Murray Coleman, "A Warrior Only By Necessity; Be Bold: Sioux Leader Sitting Bull Embodied the Finest Aspects of Indian Culture," *Investor's Business Daily*, February 9, 2004; http://news.investors.com/management-leaders-in-success/020904-395338-a-warrior-only-by-necessity-be-bold-sioux-leader-sitting-bull-embodied-the-finest-aspects-of-indian-culture.htm.

147 Os Hillman, "The God of the Valley," TGIF, Today God Is First, October 15, 2000; http://www.intheworkplace.com/apps/articles/default.asp?articleid=72671&columnid=6525.

148 Alan Axelrod, *Patton on Leadership* (Paramus NJ: Prentice Hall, 1999), 109.

149 Ibid.

150 Andy Stanley, *Next Generation Leader* (Colorado Springs: Multnomah, 2003), 133–134.

151 Frank C. Collins, *Quality: The Ball in Your Court* (Milwaukee, WI: American Society for Quality, 1994), 171–172.

152 Clifton Fadiman, *The Little Brown Book of Anecdotes* (New York: Little, Brown, 1985), 210.

153 Hal Urban, *Life's Greatest Lessons: Twenty Things That Matter* (New York: Simon & Schuster/Fireside, 2003), 122.

154 Ibid., 123.

155 Mark K. Updegrove, *Baptism by Fire* (New York: Thomas Dunne, 2008), 240.

156 *Business 2.0*, Volume 2, 2001, 57; http://www.google.com/search?hl=en&biw=1128&bih=789&q=%22Everybody%20at%20Intuit%20has%20two%20jobs%22&um=1&ie=UTF-8&tbo=u&tbm=bks&source=og&sa=N&tab=wp.

157 Stephen Ambrose Interview, "America's Time Traveler," Academy of Achievement, September 22, 2010; http://www.achievement.org/autodoc/page/amb0int-3.

158 Brian Tracy, *Focal Point* (New York: AMACOM, 2002), 78.

159 James M. Strock, *Reagan on Leadership* (Scottsdale, AZ: Serve to Lead Press, 2011), 57–58.

160 Carmine Gallo, *Ten Simple Secrets of the World's Greatest Business Communicators* (Naperville, IL: Sourcebooks, 2006), 46.

161 Bono, "Because We Can, We Must," commencement address, University of Pennsylvania, May 17, 2004; http://www.upenn.edu/almanac/between/2004/commence-b.html.

[162] Steve Jobs, commencement address, Stanford University, June 12, 2005; http://news.stanford.edu/news/2005/june15/jobs-061505.html.

[163] Aaron Sorkin, commencement address, Syracuse University, May 13, 2012; http://www.syr.edu/news/articles/2012/sorkin-remarks-05-13.html.

[164] Bill Simmons, "Appreciating the Zen Master in Full," ESPN.com, May 13, 2011; http://sports.espn.go.com/espn/page2/story?page=simmons/110513&sportCat=nba.

[165] Phil Jackson with Hugh Delehanty, *Sacred Hoops: Spiritual Lessons of a Hardwood Warrior* (New York: Hyperion, 2006), ix.

[166] PBS, "Edward R. Murrow: This Reporter," PBS.org, February 2, 2007; http://www.pbs.org/wnet/americanmasters/episodes/edward-r-murrow/this-reporter/513/.

[167] Gerardo R. Ungson and John D. Trudel, *Engines of Prosperity: Templates for the Information Age* (London: Imperial College Press, 1998), 282.

Scripture Index

Index of Names

Acknowledgments

With deep appreciation, I acknowledge the support and guidance of the following people who helped make this book possible:

Special thanks to Rich DeVos, Dan DeVos, and Alex Martins of the Orlando Magic.

Hats off to my assistant, Andrew Herdliska; my proofreader, Ken Hussar; and my ace typist, Fran Thomas.

Thanks also to my writing partner, Jim Denney, for his superb contributions in shaping this manuscript.

Hearty thanks also go to my friends at Barbour Publishing, Inc., and especially to Paul Muckley, senior editor for nonfiction, who believed in the message of this book. My thanks to the entire Barbour team—including Timothy Martins, Kelly McIntosh, Annie Tipton, Ashley Schrock, Brigitta Nortker, and Catherine Thompson—for their vision, professionalism, and skill in helping me to shape this message for publication.

And finally, special thanks and appreciation go to my wife, Ruth, and to my wonderful and supportive family. They are truly the backbone of my life.

Contact

You can contact Pat Williams at:
Pat Williams
c/o Orlando Magic
8701 Maitland Summit Boulevard
Orlando, FL 32810
phone: 407-916-2404
pwilliams@orlandomagic.com

Visit Pat Williams's website at:
www.PatWilliamsMotivate.com

If you would like to set up a speaking engagement for Pat Williams, please call or write his assistant, Andrew Herdliska, at the above address, or call him at 407-916-2401. Requests can also be faxed to 407-916-2986 or e-mailed to aherdliska@orlandomagic.com.

We would love to hear from you. Please send your comments about this book to Pat Williams at the above address. Thank you.